# the BREADHEAD BIBLE

# the BREADHEAD BIBLE

## Father Dominic's Favorite Recipes

Father Dominic Garramone, OSB

REEDY PRESS
St. Louis, Missouri

Other books by Father Dominic

To my back stage kitchen angel Bridget Kelly, without whom I would never have been a success on public television.

Reedy Press
PO Box 5131
St. Louis, MO 63139, USA
www.reedypress.com

Library of Congress Control Number: 2014935087

ISBN: 978-1-935806-66-0

Design by Jill Halpin

Printed in the United States of America
            18     5 4 3

# Contents

## All Good Grains

## Ethnic Breads

## American Flavors

## Herbal Breads

# Preface

In 1998 when a high school classmate told me that she was going to mention my name to some producers at the public television station in St. Louis, I told her she could, all the while believing that nothing was going to come of that idea. I thought: *How many people would want to watch a chubby, balding monk from a little monastery in rural Illinois host a cooking show about baking bread?* More than anyone expected, as it turned out. By 2001, *Breaking Bread with Father Dominic* was being seen by 70 percent of public television viewers, and I had written three cookbooks which had sold thousands of copies.

Those books are no longer in print (although you can still find them online and in second hand bookstores) but people still ask me for recipes from the series. So I decided to compile a collection of my favorite recipes from the three *Breaking Bread* cookbooks, along with some new recipes I've developed since then. Some of my earlier recipes I edited for clarity (and corrected a few mistakes!) and updated a few based on the new techniques and tweaks I've developed in the past decade. The result is this volume, *The Breadhead Bible*.

This cookbook is not meant to be a beginner's book, although many of the recipes are well within the reach of a novice baker, certainly in "The Basics" chapter. But I've not included introductory material about ingredients and equipment or detailed descriptions of mixing, kneading or shaping basic loaves. You can find that information in my book *How to Be a Breadhead*, as well as on my website www.breadmonk.com. Instead, I've tried to gather all the best recipes from the series in a single volume, so this can be your go-to bread book, the one that gets dog-eared and stained, with notes written in the margins and splatters on the pages of your favorite recipes.

I've tried to include photos whenever the complexity of the directions warrant it, but as my mother always said, "If you can read, you can bake." That may be a bit of an exaggeration—many people don't learn to knead dough properly without a mentor or a YouTube video—but most Breadheads shouldn't have too much difficulty following the instructions. And don't be afraid to make mistakes—I certainly didn't learn to make braided loaves without a few lopsided attempts along the way! As *Breaking Bread* viewers may remember me saying: "It's bread—it's gonna forgive you!"

God bless and happy baking!

Fr. Dominic

# The
# Basics

# Basic Biscuits

3 cups all-purpose flour
4 tsp. baking powder
1 Tbs. sugar
½ tsp. cream of tartar
½ tsp. salt

¾ cup cold butter
    (1½ sticks) cut into pieces
1 egg
1 cup milk

---

   In a medium-size bowl, combine flour, baking powder, sugar, cream of tartar, and salt; whisk until blended. Cut in butter with a pastry blender or two knives until the mixture resembles coarse crumbs. Beat egg and milk together and stir into flour mixture until just moistened. Turn dough out onto a lightly floured surface and knead about 10 strokes—do not overwork the dough or the biscuits will be tough.

Roll out to 1-inch thickness. Cut with a floured 2½-inch biscuit cutter; push scraps together and gently reroll to cut out more. Place rounds on a lightly greased baking sheet. Bake at 425°F for 12 to 15 minutes or until golden brown. Remove from pan and cool briefly on a wire rack before serving warm. Makes about a dozen.

**NOTES:**

— I never had much success with biscuits until I came across a recipe which suggested adding some cream of tartar to the dry ingredients. Sure enough, that did the trick for me—victory at last!—although I'm sure there are plenty of biscuit purists out there who will scoff at the idea. Try it and decide for yourself. I often refer to them as "Biscuits of Victory," spoken in an epic voice with trumpets in the background.

— It is absolutely essential that you have a sharp biscuit cutter, or the act of cutting out the biscuit will seal the edges and they won't rise or be as flaky. Cut straight down and don't twist the cutter for the same reason.

— You can have a batch of biscuits made in 30 minutes. So why not wake up a little earlier this Sunday and treat the family to the aroma of fresh baked biscuits. I doubt anyone will sleep in!

# Basic Roll Dough

2 pkg. active dry yeast
¼ cup lukewarm water
    (100 to 110°F)
2 cups 2% milk
¼ cup (½ stick) butter

¼ cup sugar
2 tsp. salt
2 eggs, lightly beaten
5 to 5½ cups flour

---

In a small bowl, proof yeast in the water. Heat milk in a saucepan, but do not boil. Add butter, sugar, and salt to milk; mix well and cool to lukewarm. Pour into a medium-size mixing bowl along with proofed yeast and the 2 beaten eggs. Add 2 cups of flour and beat until smooth. Add 2 more cups of flour, 1 at a time, and mix with a heavy spoon until the flour is fully incorporated. Add 1 more cup of flour and mix with your hands until it is incorporated. Remove from bowl and turn out onto a lightly floured surface and knead for 5 minutes, adding more flour as needed to form a smooth, elastic dough—remember that dough for rolls should be slightly softer than most bread dough.

Place in a greased bowl and let rise, covered, in a warm place free from drafts until doubled, about 1 to 1½ hours. Punch down dough and knead for 2 minutes to work out air bubbles. Let rest for 10 minutes. Then shape into desired rolls and let rise again until doubled, about 30 minutes. Preheat oven to 400°F. Bake until golden brown, about 12 to 15 minutes.
Makes 20 to 24 rolls.

## Cloverleaf Rolls

Lightly grease muffin tins. Roll dough into small balls, about the size of a walnut. Place 3 balls in each muffin tin. Allow to rise until doubled and bake as directed.

## Crescent Rolls

See page 12 for instructions.

## Butter Fantans

Roll dough out about ¼-inch thick and brush the top with melted butter. Cut dough into strips about 2 inches wide. Stack five strips on top of one another. Using a sharp knife, cut the layered strips into individual stacks. Place each stack, cut side down, into greased muffin tins. Let rise, covered, until nearly doubled. Bake as directed.

## Bow Knots

Roll individual pieces of dough into ropes 8 to 10 inches long, about ½-inch thick. Form each rope into a knot, and place on a lightly greased cookie sheet. Cover and let rise; bake as directed.

**NOTES:**
— If you want rolls with a slightly chewier crust, roll balls and place them in a lightly greased muffin tin. For buns with soft sides, use a 9 x 13 inch baking pan.

— This same dough makes lovely cinnamon rolls.

# Basic Wheat Bread

2 pkg. active dry yeast
2¼ cups lukewarm water
   (100 to 110°F)
2 Tbs. brown sugar

2 Tbs. vegetable oil
2 tsp. salt
2 cups whole wheat flour
3½ to 4 cups bread flour

Dissolve yeast in warm water in a large mixing bowl. Add sugar, oil, and salt, and mix well. Add wheat flour and mix well until flour is thoroughly incorporated. Allow batter to rest for 5 minutes to allow the wheat flour to absorb more liquid. Add 3 cups of white flour, 1 cup at a time, mixing thoroughly after each cup. Turn dough out onto a lightly floured countertop. Knead for 8 to 10 minutes, adding more flour as needed to make a smooth and elastic dough that is only slightly sticky. Lightly oil the surface of the dough and place in a clean, dry bowl. Cover with a dry cloth and let rise about an hour or until doubled.

Punch down dough and knead briefly to expel larger air bubbles. Divide dough into two equal portions. Lightly dust your hands with flour. Grasp the

first portion of dough on opposite sides and pull gently to stretch the top. Tuck the ends under and pinch them gently. Give the dough a quarter turn and repeat, again stretching the top into a smooth surface; tuck the ends under and pinch. Repeat as necessary to form a smooth round of dough with some tension on the top. This tight surface will hold the gases better and make for a higher, lighter loaf. Repeat with the other portion of dough. You may also roll the dough gently on the countertop under your palm to form an oval shape.

Place the loaves on a lightly greased baking sheet, evenly spaced. Cover with a clean, dry cloth and let rise for 30 minutes or until almost doubled. Using a very sharp knife, slash a cross into the top of each loaf just before placing them in the oven. Bake in a preheated 375°F oven on the middle rack for 20 to 25 minutes, or until loaves are lightly browned and sound hollow when tapped. The interior temperature of the loaf should be 195 to 200°F. Cool on a wire rack.

## NOTES:

— Because whole wheat flour has proportionally less protein by volume than white flours, bread flour is recommended for this recipe to increase the amount of gluten in the dough. Otherwise, the resulting loaf may be rather dense and heavy. There's some extra kneading involved compared to other bread recipes for the same reason. It's worth the effort.

— You can substitute granulated sugar, molasses, or honey for the brown sugar. You can also follow the instructions for baking in loaf pans; see Basic White Bread on page 8.

— I make this bread every year on Holy Thursday, often with my students. One year we baked over 50 loaves of wheat bread for a bake sale to benefit the hurricane victims in Haiti. We sold out of bread in 13 minutes!

# Basic White Bread

2 pkg. active dry yeast
2 cups lukewarm water
   (100 to 110°F)
2 Tbs. granulated sugar

2 Tbs. vegetable oil
2 tsp. salt
5½ to 6 cups all-purpose flour

---

Dissolve yeast in warm water in a large mixing bowl. Add sugar, oil, and salt, and mix well. Add 5 cups of flour, 1 cup at a time, mixing well after each cup. Knead for 5 to 8 minutes, adding more flour as needed to make a smooth and elastic dough that is only slightly sticky. Lightly oil the surface of the dough and place in a clean, dry bowl. Cover with a dry cloth and let rise about an hour or until doubled.

Punch the dough down, and knead it lightly to expel larger air bubbles. Divide dough in half and shape into loaves. Place in lightly greased 8½ × 4½ × 2½ inch loaf pans; cover with a clean, dry cloth and let rise for 30 minutes or until nearly doubled. Bake in a preheated 400°F oven on the middle rack for 35 minutes, or until loaves are lightly browned and sound hollow when tapped. The interior temperature of the loaf should be between 190 and 195°F. Remove from pans and cool on a wire rack.

## NOTES:

— There are lots of variations on this basic white bread regarding the amount of water, sugar, salt, and oil. For example, my mother's favorite version uses half water and half milk and includes a quarter cup of oil. I like my recipe because everything's in "twos" except the flour, so it's easy to carry the recipe in your head.

— You could use bread flour in place of the all-purpose flour in this recipe and get bread with greater loft and lightness. However, bread flour absorbs more liquid than all-purpose, so use less flour or your loaf could be dry. It's always better to err on the side of sticky than to add too much flour.

— You could add a tablespoon or two of dried herbs to this recipe to make an herb bread. Choose herbs that will complement the flavors of the rest of your meal.

# The Classics

# Best Ever Crescent Rolls

2 pkg. active dry yeast
½ cup lukewarm water
    (100 to 110°F)
1 cup milk (skim, 2%, or
    whole milk all OK)
¼ cup sugar

1½ tsp. salt
1 cup mashed potatoes
2 large eggs, beaten
6 to 6½ cups all-purpose flour
⅓ cup shortening, melted and
    cooled to lukewarm

Proof the yeast by mixing it in a small bowl with the warm water and allowing it to develop for 5 minutes. Heat milk in a saucepan, but do not boil. Add sugar and salt, mix well, and cool to lukewarm. Pour into a five-quart mixing bowl and stir in the mashed potatoes, proofed yeast, and eggs until smooth. One cup at a time, add 4 cups of flour, mixing thoroughly each time until the flour is incorporated. Beat in the melted shortening. Add another 1½ cups of flour, and mix with your hands until the dough pulls away from the side of the bowl and forms a single mass. Remove from the bowl and turn out onto a lightly floured surface and knead for 5 or 6 minutes, adding more flour as needed to form a smooth, elastic dough. Remember that dough for rolls should be slightly softer than most bread dough. Place in a greased bowl and let rise, covered, in a warm place free from drafts until doubled, 1 to 1½ hours. Punch down dough and knead briefly to expel the larger air bubbles.

Divide dough into three portions and shape into smooth rounds. Cover with a clean, dry cloth and let rest 10 minutes to allow the gluten strands to relax so it will be easier to roll out. Roll one portion of dough into a circle roughly 14 inches in diameter. With a small pizza cutter or sharp knife, cut into eight equal wedges. Starting with the wide end of each triangle, roll up and curve the pointed ends to shape into a crescent. Note that the points are curved toward the narrower side of the top layer of dough and the point of the dough ends up on the bottom of the roll. Place the rolls,

evenly spaced, on lightly greased cookie sheets—allow room for them to nearly double in volume. Cover baking sheet with a clean, dry cloth. Repeat with remaining portions of dough. Allow to rise until nearly doubled in a warm place, free from drafts—30 to 45 minutes. Bake at 375°F until lightly browned, about 12 minutes (the interior temperature of the rolls should be 190 to 195°F). Remove rolls from pan to cool slightly on wire racks and serve warm.

**NOTES:**

— When I make dinner rolls, I want rolls so light that they hover a scant sixteenth of an inch above the wire rack while cooling. I decided that the best way to develop such a recipe was to research recipes that were winners at state fairs. Almost every roll that was a county fair favorite, a state 4-H winner, or "best ever" recipe had some similar characteristics: an extra egg, shortening rather than butter, and the addition of mashed potatoes to the dough.

— This same dough can be used for other rolls, buns, and coffee cakes.

# Cinnamon Swirl Bread

Dough
2 pkg. active dry yeast
¼ cup lukewarm water
   (100 to 110°F)
1 cup milk
1 cup sour cream
3 Tbs. shortening or butter
¼ cup sugar
1 Tbs. vanilla extract

2 tsp. salt
3 eggs
5½ to 6½ cups all-purpose flour

Filling
2 Tbs. butter, melted
¼ cup sugar
2 Tbs. cinnamon
pinch of nutmeg

Proof yeast in water. Place milk, sour cream, and shortening in a saucepan over low heat until sour cream and shortening are melted and combined. Remove from heat and cool to lukewarm. In a large bowl, combine milk mixture, sugar, yeast, vanilla, salt, and eggs, mixing well. Add 2 cups of flour and beat to incorporate. Add 2 more cups, mixing thoroughly. About a half cup at a time, add enough of the remaining flour to make a soft dough that pulls away from the side of the bowl. Turn out onto a lightly floured board and knead for 5 minutes, adding small amounts of flour as needed to keep the dough manageable. The result should be a smooth, elastic dough that is not stiff. Lightly oil the surface of the dough, place in a clean, dry bowl and cover with a clean cloth. Let rise in a warm place free from drafts until it doubles, 1 to 1½ hours.

Combine sugar and spices for filling in a small bowl. Punch down dough and knead for 2 minutes to work out the bubbles. Divide into two parts. On a lightly floured board or pastry cloth, roll each section of dough into a rectangle about 14 x 7 inches. Spread with melted butter, and sprinkle on the sugar filling, leaving a ½-inch border of "clean dough" on all edges. Starting with the shorter edge, roll dough up tightly and seal the edges.

Place in greased 9 × 5 inch pans. Cover with a towel and let rise until nearly doubled, about 45 to 60 minutes. Bake in a preheated oven at 375°F for 35 to 45 minutes—loosely cover the loaves with aluminum foil if the tops begin browning too quickly. Remove from pans and cool on a rack. If desired, while the loaves are still warm, brush the top with butter and sprinkle with cinnamon sugar.

## NOTES:

— This bread makes excellent toast, which as far as I am concerned is the quintessential after-school snack.

— Be careful not to add too much flour, either in mixing or kneading, or the dough will be too stiff to roll out. It's better for the dough to be a bit too soft than too stiff.

— When sealing the edges of the loaf, brush the edge of the dough with a little milk if you have trouble getting it to stick.

# Cottage Loaf

2 pkg. active dry yeast
2 cups lukewarm water
    (100 to 110°F)
2 Tbs. honey
3 cups whole wheat flour

¼ cup nonfat dry milk
3 Tbs. canola oil
2 tsp. salt
3½ to 4 cups bread flour

In a medium-size bowl, combine yeast with warm water and honey, and stir until completely dissolved. Add whole wheat flour, dry milk, gluten, oil, and salt; stir until thoroughly blended. Add 3 cups of bread flour, 1 cup at a time, mixing each time until the flour is completely incorporated. About ¼ cup at a time, work in enough of remaining flour to form a fairly stiff dough. Knead for 6 to 8 minutes. Oil the surface of the dough and place in a clean, dry bowl. Cover with a clean cloth and let rise in a warm place free from drafts for about 1 hour, or until doubled in volume.

Punch dough down and knead briefly to expel larger air bubbles—let rest for 5 minutes. Divide dough into two portions with about ⅔ and ⅓ of the dough, respectively. Form each piece into a smooth ball and place on a lightly floured surface and cover with a clean, dry towel. Let rise for 20 minutes. Lightly grease a large baking sheet and sprinkle it with cornmeal. Carefully place the larger piece in the center of the baking sheet and brush the top lightly with water or milk. Place the smaller piece on top and use the handle of a wooden spoon dusted with flour to push down through the center to make the two pieces stick together. Allow to rise another 20 minutes. Bake in a preheated 375°F oven for 50 to 55 minutes, or until crust is browned and loaf sounds hollow when tapped on the bottom. Cool on wire rack.

## NOTES:

— The cottage loaf shape can be used for any bread, wheat or white. The shape originated in Britain during the Roman occupation, when ovens were rather tall and shaped like beehives. To stack one loaf on top of another made maximum use of oven space, a necessity when the ovens were communal and had to accommodate all the bakers in the village.

— I find it's best to bake this loaf by time rather than appearance, as often the surface browns quickly and even the "tap on the bottom" test makes you think the bread is done, but the loaf is so large it may still be doughy in the center. It won't hurt to leave the bread in an extra five minutes, but taking it out too early may yield disappointing results. If you are using an instant-read thermometer, the bread is completely baked when the interior reaches at least 195°F.

# Elegant Soda Bread

4 cups all-purpose flour
1 tsp. baking soda
2 tsp. baking powder
2 tsp. salt

¼ cup sugar
1½ tsp. ground coriander
2 cups buttermilk

---

Preheat oven to 375°F. Sift dry ingredients into a medium-size bowl. Gradually add buttermilk, stirring until smooth. The dough will be quite soft—do not overmix. Divide dough in half, and using floured hands, form each half into a round, slightly flattened shape. Place in greased pie plates and cut a cross in the top to keep it from splitting during baking. Bake at 375°F for 45 to 60 minutes, or until bread sounds hollow when tapped both top and bottom. Remove from pans to cool on wire racks. While loaves are still hot, you may brush the tops with butter.

## NOTES:

— When I was in my first year of priestly studies at St. Meinrad School of Theology, I used to visit Louisville, Kentucky, about 70 miles away. In my first trip there with my friend John, we found a guide of the top 60 restaurants in the city. We decided that we would attempt to eat our way through the guide over the next four years (leaving out anyplace that required dressing up too much!). Of course, we never got past the first 20, because we found a few we really liked and stuck with them. One of these favorites was a classy but unpretentious place called Jack Fry's on Bardstown Road. They served a coriander soda bread with every entree, and I used to eat baskets of it. The addition of coriander gives the bread an undercurrent of citrus that is subtle and exquisite.

— If you omit the coriander, reduce the sugar to 2 teaspoons, and add a 15-ounce package of raisins, you'd have my mother's favorite Irish soda bread recipe. She got it from Mrs. Jones, the mother of a priest who taught my mom in high school in Denver. Mom used to make this for the bake sale at St. Francis Hospital, which was always held the week before St. Patrick's Day. She'd tie a green ribbon through the cross, to make it more attractive for the sale table. But she needn't have bothered—the people working behind the counter often bought it right out of her hand!

# Fabs' Nutty Goodness Rolls

## Dough
2 pkg. yeast
½ cup lukewarm water
   (100 to 110°F)
1½ cups sour cream
2 Tbs. vegetable oil
½ cup sugar
¼ tsp. baking soda
2 tsp. salt
2 large eggs
4½ cups flour

## Filling
⅓ cup packed brown sugar
⅓ cup granulated sugar
¼ cup all-purpose flour
1 Tbs. ground cinnamon
¼ cup (½ stick) cold butter, cut
   into small pieces
½ cup chopped pecans

In a small bowl, proof yeast in the water. Warm sour cream, vegetable oil, and sugar in a saucepan over medium heat—do not boil. Remove from heat and cool to lukewarm. Stir in soda and salt, then cool to lukewarm. Pour into large bowl, and add yeast and eggs, stirring until smooth. Add flour, about 1 cup at a time. Turn out onto lightly floured board and knead for 3 to 5 minutes. Dough will be rather sticky, but avoid the temptation to add too much more flour, just a tablespoon or two to keep the dough manageable. Allow dough to rest for about 10 minutes (it will firm up nicely during this time). In a small bowl, prepare filling by combining brown sugar, granulated sugar, flour, cinnamon, and butter; blend together with a pastry mixer or two knives until the mixture resembles coarse crumbs. Stir in the pecans. Prepare caramel sauce as directed on next page.

Roll dough out into an 18 × 16 inch rectangle. Sprinkle with filling. Roll up from long side, jellyroll style, and pinch to seal the edge (brush the edge with a little water if necessary to make it stick). Pour caramel sauce into the bottom of a lightly greased 9 × 13 × 2 inch pan and sprinkle with the remaining ¾ cup of nuts. Cut dough crosswise into 12 rolls and place, cut side down, into the prepared pan. Cover and let rise for 45 to 60 minutes, or

until nearly doubled. Place pan on a jellyroll pan to catch any drips, and bake in a preheated 375°F oven for 30 to 35 minutes. Invert onto serving plate while still warm.

<u>Nutty Goodness Caramel Sauce</u>

Combine ½ cup (1 stick) butter, 1 cup brown sugar, and ¼ cup corn syrup in a small saucepan, and cook over medium heat just until sugar is dissolved. Remove from heat and cool slightly.

NOTES:

— I cannot make these rolls often enough for my students. Once when I was mixing the filling, one of the alumni, Jason "Fabs" Fabish, looked at the bowl of sugar and butter and nuts for the filling and exclaimed in a whisper, "Ohhhhhhhh—nutty goodness!" We have called them "Fabs' Nutty Goodness" ever since.

— When you first mix the dough, it will seem much too moist and sticky, but the 10-minute rest really does make it firm up. If the weather is extremely humid and your kitchen isn't air-conditioned, you may add up to another ½ cup of flour during mixing, but no more.

# Hero Sandwich Bread

2 pkg. active dry yeast
1½ cups lukewarm water
   (100 to 110°F)
½ cup sugar

3 Tbs. vegetable oil
2 tsp. salt
1 egg
5-6 cups all-purpose flour

---

    Dissolve yeast in warm water in a large mixing bowl. Add sugar, oil, salt, and egg and mix well. Add 5 cups of flour, 1 cup at a time, mixing well after each cup. Knead for 5 to 8 minutes, adding more flour as needed to make a fairly soft dough. Put in greased bowl and turn over. Cover and let rise about an hour until doubled. Punch down, knead, cover, and let rise again for 45 minutes. Punch down, knead again, and form into two long loaves, slightly flattened, or four thinner loaves on two pans. Place loaves on a lightly greased 12 × 18 inch jellyroll pan. Cover with a towel and let rise until almost doubled, about 30 minutes. Bake for 22 to 25 minutes at 350°F.

## NOTES:

— As far as I'm concerned, the very best hero sandwich is the "Gondola" made at Avanti's in Peoria, which was one of our favorite hangout places after high school football and basketball games. Avanti's bread is legendary in central Illinois, and the recipe is a well-kept secret. I have seen several different pirated versions of it, but as is so often the case, nothing you produce in your kitchen can equal the real thing. But here's my modest attempt, which I have developed after extensive experimentation, the samples of which were eagerly devoured by the stage crew of our Academy theatre department. Thinly sliced salami and boiled ham, American cheese, and lettuce are the classic Gondola toppings, but just about anything you put on this bread will be delicious.

— Because of the relatively large amount of sugar, this bread will darken more quickly than other breads, so keep a careful eye on it while baking, and rotate the pans to prevent uneven browning. The crust will be fairly thin, and the texture will be very fine and quite soft because of the eggs. Be sure to knead the dough thoroughly, so that the bread will hold together under the pressure of your toppings.

# Honey Oatmeal Bread

1 cup rolled oats
2 cups hot water
2 pkg. active dry yeast
¼ cup lukewarm water
    (100 to 110°F)
⅓ cup honey

2 tsp. salt
1 Tbs. butter or oil
5½ cups of all-purpose flour,
    approx.
extra oatmeal for coating

Put the oats in a large bowl. Bring 2 cups water to a boil, pour over the oats, and stir—let stand to cool to lukewarm. Stir the yeast into warm water and let stand for 5 minutes to dissolve. Feel the oats at the bottom of the bowl to be sure they're lukewarm, then add the honey, salt, butter, and dissolved yeast. Work in enough of the flour so that the dough can be handled, but remember that the oatmeal and the honey will make this a very sticky dough. Turn out onto a lightly floured board, knead for a minute or 2, and then let rest for 10 minutes. Resume kneading until the dough is elastic, but still rather sticky—don't add too much flour at a time. Lightly oil the surface of the dough and place in a clean bowl. Cover with a clean, dry cloth and let rise in a warm spot until double in bulk.

Punch dough down and divide into two pieces. Knead each piece to remove the large air bubbles, but do not use any flour on the kneading board—you want the dough to remain sticky. Roll each loaf in the extra oatmeal until it is completely covered and shape into loaves. Place loaves in medium loaf pans and allow to rise until nearly doubled, about 30 minutes. Bake in a preheated 350°F oven for 40 to 45 minutes. The interior temperature should be between 195 and 200°F. Remove from pans and cool on racks.

## NOTES:

— I love oatmeal bread, and the extra oatmeal coating on this bread makes it especially good. The dough will be somewhat stickier than other doughs, so be careful not to add too much flour. This bread is very chewy, and is excellent toasted. This recipe is a monastery favorite, and it sells quickly at bake sales because of its beautiful appearance.

— Doughs made with honey may darken more quickly than other breads. If the loaves start to get too dark, cover them loosely with aluminum foil and continue baking.

— For an excellent low-fat sandwich, use this bread with fresh garden tomatoes and smoked turkey; no need for cheese or dressing for added flavor.

# Hot Cross Buns

1 pkg. fast-rising yeast
1 tsp. cinnamon
¼ tsp. nutmeg
¼ cup sugar
1¼ tsp. salt
½ cup whole wheat flour

4 to 4½ cups white bread flour
1 cup milk
½ cup butter
2 beaten eggs
¾ cup raisins

---

Put yeast, spices, sugar, and salt in a mixing bowl with whole wheat flour and 2 cups of bread flour and stir until thoroughly blended. Warm milk in a saucepan with butter over low heat until butter melts; cool mixture to just above lukewarm (120 to 130°F). Add milk mixture to the dry ingredients and beat for 200 strokes. Add the eggs, and mix until well blended. Stir in the raisins. About half a cup at a time, add two more cups of bread flour and mix until it is incorporated. Turn dough out onto a floured board and knead lightly, adding enough of the remaining flour to make a soft dough. Knead for about 5 minutes, until the dough is smooth and elastic. Rub the surface of the dough lightly with oil or butter, and place in a clean bowl. Cover and let rise in a warm place free from drafts until doubled, about 1 to 1½ hours.

Punch dough down and put onto a floured board; knead lightly to remove air bubbles. Divide into 12 pieces and form bun shapes, tucking sides under to avoid spreading. Place buns on a lightly greased cookie sheet, and cover with a towel to let rise for about 45 minutes to an hour. Preheat oven to 375°F. When buns have risen to nearly double in size, use a sharp knife or razor blade to mark a deep cross in each. Bake for 15 to 20 minutes. Remove the buns from the pan and place them on a wire rack. Allow to cool for 15 minutes, then brush on the glaze. Serve warm.

## Glaze

¾ cup powdered sugar, 2 Tbs. milk, 1 Tbs. melted butter, ¼ tsp. vanilla. Beat until smooth. Use a pastry brush to apply the glaze to the still-warm buns. You may also add more powdered sugar to make a thicker frosting to pipe a cross on the top of each bun.

**NOTES:**

— I dislike the look of store-bought hot cross buns with yellow frosting piped on top. The traditional Irish form is made with a cross cut in the top of the bun, a custom going back to pagan times.

— These sweet buns can be made with currants or dried cherries as well.

— My community likes these so much I have to make them three times a year: for Ash Wednesday, Good Friday, and the Seventh Sunday of Easter. I'm just imitating my Irish grandma Tootsie (maiden name McNulty) who made them several times a year for my Austrian grandfather.

# Kaiser Rolls

2 pkg. active dry yeast
1 cup lukewarm water
    (100 to 110°F)
1 Tbs. barley malt syrup
1 cup lukewarm milk
1 Tbs. vegetable oil

1 Tbs. salt
1 egg, separated
6 to 6½ cups all-purpose flour
sesame or poppy seeds
    (optional)

---

In a medium-size bowl, combine yeast with warm water and stir until completely dissolved. Stir in malt syrup and allow to sit for 10 minutes. Add milk, oil, salt, and egg yolk; stir until thoroughly blended. Add 6 cups of flour, 1 cup at a time, mixing each time until the flour is completely incorporated. Turn dough out onto a lightly floured surface and knead for 6 to 8 minutes, adding small amount of flour as needed to keep the dough manageable. Oil the surface of the dough and place in a clean bowl. Cover with a clean, dry dish towel and let rise in a warm place free from drafts for about 1 hour, or until doubled in volume.

Punch dough down and knead briefly to expel larger air bubbles. Divide dough into 12 equal pieces. Lightly grease a 12 × 18 inch baking sheet. Roll each piece of dough into a ball, then flatten into a circle 3 to 4 inches across (dust the surface of the dough lightly with flour to keep it from sticking to your hands). Place rolls on the baking sheet, evenly spaced, and cover with a clean, dry dish towel. Let rise in a warm place free from drafts for 20 minutes. Uncover, and press each roll firmly with a Kaiser roll stamp (the stamp should lightly touch the pan beneath the roll). Let rise, uncovered, for another 10 minutes. Combine egg white with 2 Tbs. water. Brush rolls with egg wash, and sprinkle with sesame or poppy seeds if desired. Bake in a preheated 375°F oven on the middle rack for 20 minutes, or until lightly browned evenly on top. Remove from pan and cool on racks. Makes 12 rolls.

## NOTES:

— This recipe became an instant favorite with many of the brethren, especially Fr. Ronald, who eats a rather Spartan breakfast of toasted roll and coffee each morning and is always on the lookout for decent breads.

— I have seen several different versions of Kaiser roll recipes, one of which calls for three egg whites. I hate recipes that leave you with extra egg yolks or half a can of something that's just going to go bad in the fridge. So for my version I put the egg yolk in the dough and use the white to wash the crust. Besides, it's the barley malt syrup that gives Kaiser rolls their unique flavor and texture. It may be a bit difficult to locate if you don't have a health food store nearby. Dark corn syrup is a decent substitute, or 2 teaspoons of brown sugar with a teaspoon of molasses.

— Kaiser rolls get their name and shape from the crown of the German kaiser—early versions of the rolls were twisted by hand rather than shaped with a stamp. You may have a little trouble locating a Kaiser roll stamp, but a culinary store can order you one if they don't have it in stock. The plastic ones work just fine, and generally cost less than $10. The stamp will make the classic five-armed swirl on top the roll, and as a nice surprise, a smaller star on the bottom of the roll as well.

# Popovers

1 cup all-purpose flour
½ tsp. salt
1 cup milk or buttermilk
2 eggs

1 Tbs. melted butter
6 small pieces of butter (about
   ½ tsp. each)

---

Bring all ingredients to room temperature. Preheat oven to 425°F. In a one-quart bowl, mix together flour and salt. In a separate bowl, beat together milk, eggs, and melted butter. Gradually pour egg mixture into dry ingredients, stirring constantly. Beat until smooth (I like to use a small whisk) and set aside. Place a small piece of butter in the bottom of each section of the popover pan. Place in oven until butter is bubbling, about 1 minute. Remove pan from oven and divide batter between the 6 sections of the pan (about ⅔ cup in each). Bake for 20 minutes (don't open the oven to peek or the popovers will fall), then lower the temperature to 325°F and bake for another 10 minutes. Remove from oven and prick the top of each popover with a fork a couple of times. Bake for another 5 minutes—popovers will be golden brown and rather firm on top. Remove from oven and allow to cool in the pan for about 10 minutes before removing popovers. Serve warm with butter and honey.

## NOTES:

— Popovers are making a comeback these days. I first learned about popovers from a delightful Irish lady named Kate, who was working as the housekeeper at a parish where I was substituting one weekend. She served me fresh popovers at supper, and I became an instant fan. I asked her for her secret, and she confided in a near whisper: "You have to bring the ingredients to room temperature before you mix a thing, or they just won't pop." She wrote down her exact recipe for me, which I have since lost (oh, Mona!) but her advice remains with me as the key to perfect popovers.

— Popovers are versatile breads and are delicious in any number of ways. Among my studio interns from season three, Keith slathers his with butter and honey, David prefers his with grape jelly, and Chris cuts off the top and fills it with chocolate pudding. They can be served hot, filled with shrimp in a garlic cream sauce, or cold with herbed cheese spread.

# Pull Apart Garlic Bread

1 batch of Basic White Bread
  dough (see page 8)
½ cup melted butter
  (NOT diet spread)
2 Tbs. dried parsley
  (use 3 Tbs. if fresh)

1 Tbs. Italian seasoning mix
1 Tbs. granulated garlic
  (more if stronger garlic flavor
  is desired)
2 Tbs. beaten egg

Mix all ingredients in a bowl. For each loaf, divide dough into 12 pieces, and dip each piece into the butter mixture, coating completely. Arrange in a single layer—you'll have to squish them a little—in a 9 × 5 inch greased loaf pan. Pour any remaining butter over the two loaves. Let rise until the dough just reaches the top of the pan, then bake at 375°F for about 45 minutes. About 10 minutes before the bread is done, you can brush the tops with some of the remaining beaten egg and sprinkle the tops with Parmesan cheese. Remove from pans and serve warm.

## NOTES:

— Sometimes the butter mixture will spill out of the pans, so I set them on a cookie sheet to catch any drips. Otherwise you have to clean the bottom of the oven, and in an electric oven there can be a danger of fire (this is a matter of personal experience!).

— If you have leftovers (not very likely!), reheat in a conventional oven, NOT the microwave. This is a good general rule for all homemade breads, because the crust gets tough after microwaving.

— The Stage Rats really like this bread with Italian beef, and each year they eat about 6 loaves at our Christmas party.

# Raisin Bread

2 pkg. active dry yeast
¼ cup lukewarm water
    (100 to 110°F)
1½ cups milk
3 Tbs. butter
2 Tbs. sugar

2 tsp. salt
2 eggs
5½ to 6 cups bread flour
1½ cups raisins
extra butter and sugar
    for topping

---

    Proof yeast in warm water. In a small saucepan, heat milk and butter until butter is nearly melted. Pour into a large mixing bowl and cool to lukewarm. Add yeast, sugar, salt, and eggs, and stir until blended. Add 5 cups of flour, 1 cup at a time, until the dough is workable and pulls away from the side of the bowl. Add the raisins and mix them in by hand. Turn dough out onto a lightly floured board and knead for 5 minutes, adding enough of the remaining flour to make a smooth, elastic dough. Place in large bowl and cover with a dish towel. Let rise in a warm place free from drafts for about 1 hour.

    Punch dough down and knead briefly to work out larger air bubbles. Form into 2 loaves and place in greased pans. Let rise until nearly doubled, about 45 minutes. Brush the top of each loaf with melted butter and sprinkle with sugar. Bake at 425°F for 10 minutes. Then loosely cover loaves with aluminum foil and reduce heat to 375°F. Bake for another 25 to 30 minutes. Loaves are done when they sound hollow when tapped on the bottom. Remove from pans and cool on racks.

**NOTES:**

— This is another one of Mom's favorite recipes, which has won a ribbon no fewer than 21 times at the Heart of Illinois Fair. I can't guarantee you a blue ribbon, but you'll be a winner with your family and friends if you bake raisin bread. The sugar topping forms a beautiful brown crust, and the milk makes for a soft, tender crumb.

— I will be the first to admit that I don't make this bread as often as my fellow monks would like. It makes exquisite toast.

# Shortcut Croissants

1 cup (2 sticks) chilled butter,
    cut into ½-inch slices
3½ cups flour, divided (plus flour
    for dusting)
1 pkg. fast-rising yeast

2 Tbs. sugar
½ tsp. salt
1 cup milk
1 egg, lightly beaten

In a medium-size bowl, toss butter into 1½ cups flour until all the pieces are coated with flour, then blend briefly using a pastry blender or two knives. Butter pieces should be larger than for pie crust, about the size of lima beans. Place butter mixture in the refrigerator while you make the dough. In another medium-size bowl, combine yeast with sugar, salt, and remaining 2 cups of flour and stir until well blended. Heat milk to 120 to 130°F and pour into flour mixture. Beat until smooth. Stir in the egg, then beat for 2 or 3 minutes by hand. Let batter rest for 15 minutes. Stir batter down and add the butter mixture. Stir until well blended, then cover the bowl with plastic wrap and refrigerate for at least 2 hours.

On a well-floured board or pastry cloth, roll dough out into an 18 × 12 inch rectangle—the dough will be lumpy because of the butter pieces. Fold one third over the center of the dough, and the remaining third over that, so you have a triple-decker package that is 6 × 12 inches. Line up the edges carefully and press them together. Turn the package with the 6-inch side directly in front of you and dust the top with flour. Again roll the dough out to 12 inches wide and 18 inches tall. Fold again into a triple-decker and turn again. Repeat this process—roll out, fold, turn—3 more times, keeping the work surface and the dough well-dusted with flour as you work. Wrap the dough loosely in a layer of parchment or waxed paper, then in a layer of plastic wrap, and refrigerate for at least 1 hour, or overnight.

Divide dough in half. On a well-floured board or pastry cloth, roll 1 portion of dough out into a 13 × 13 inch square. Trim dough to 12 × 12 inches. Using a pizza cutter or sharp knife, cut dough into 2 rectangles. Cut out elongated triangles. Starting from the 3-inch side, roll each triangle loosely toward the point. Place point side down on an ungreased baking sheet and curve ends to form a croissant. Repeat with remaining portion of dough, using a second baking sheet as needed. (The trimmings can be tied into loose knots as baker's samples.) Cover with a light cloth and let rise until doubled, 45 to 60 minutes. If desired, brush croissants with an egg wash (one egg beaten together with 2 tablespoons warm water). Bake in a preheated 400°F oven for 10 minutes or until golden brown. Remove from baking sheets and cool on wire racks. Makes 28 small croissants.

NOTES:
— Despite the long directions, this recipe really is a time saver compared to making full-blown pastry, because the butter is cut into the flour, and you don't need to chill the dough every time you roll it out. These are not quite as flaky as genuine croissants, but far better than ordinary crescent rolls.

— These little rolls are meant to be served at breakfast with honey, or at tea with homemade apricot preserves, but NOT as a base for sandwiches. If you are going to the trouble to bake homemade croissants, don't spoil them by covering their delicate flavors with spicy lunch meats. After all the effort to make your rolls puff up, why squish them flat as a sandwich?

# All Good Grains

# Anna's Honey Bread

1½ cups whole wheat flour
¼ cup quick cooking oats
¼ cup rye flour
¼ cup wheat germ
¼ cup wheat bran
2 tsp. salt

2 pkg. active dry yeast
2 cups milk
½ cup light honey
¼ cup vegetable oil
1 egg, lightly beaten
3 to 3½ cups bread flour

In a large mixing bowl, combine whole wheat flour, oats, rye flour, wheat germ, wheat bran, salt, and yeast; mix well. In a saucepan, heat milk, honey, and oil to 130°F. Stir into dry mixture and beat for 2 minutes, then add egg and beat for 1 minute more. Let the batter rest for 5 minutes as the various grains absorb moisture.

Add 3 cups of bread flour, 1 cup at a time, mixing thoroughly after each addition. Turn dough out onto a lightly floured surface and knead for 3 minutes, adding small amounts of the remaining flour to keep the dough manageable. Cover the dough with a clean, dry dish towel and allow to rest

If you don't have any wheat germ or bran, you can substitute crushed bran cereal. The oats, rye flour, and honey combine to make an unusually sticky dough, so resist the temptation to add more flour than is absolutely necessary to keep the dough from sticking to your hands. Don't push downward too hard as you knead and you'll have an easier time of it.

for 5 minutes, again as the flours absorb the moisture. After the resting period, knead the dough for another 5 to 7 minutes. The resulting dough should be sticky but not gooey, firm but not stiff. Lightly oil the surface of the dough and place it in the rinsed mixing bowl. Cover with a towel and let rise in a warm, draft-free place for 60 to 90 minutes, or until doubled in bulk.

Punch down dough and knead briefly to work out the larger air bubbles. Divide dough in half and form into loaves. Place loaves in lightly greased 8½ × 4 ½ × 2½ inch loaf pans. Cover with a towel and let rise for 30 to 45 minutes or until nearly doubled in bulk.

Preheat oven to 350°F. Bake 40 to 45 minutes or until loaves are dark brown and sound hollow when tapped. The interior temperature of the bread should be about 200°F. Remove from pans and let cool on wire racks.

## NOTES:

— Sometime after the airing of our first season of *Breaking Bread*, a woman named Anna Druelinger sent me several recipes, including one for multigrain bread that she developed back in 1976, and very kindly anticipated that I might make use of it by adding at the bottom of the page: "You have my approval to use these recipes as you desire." I have adapted her original recipe slightly, and scaled it down to produce two loaves instead of four.

— Our Fr. Marion of happy memory was one of the biggest fans of my multigrain breads, especially toasted for breakfast. He would pass up any number of coffeecakes, pastries, and doughnuts for the sake of toasted wheat bread with butter and honey. This bread already has plenty of honey flavor, so butter alone may be just right. I specify light honey in the recipe; if you have honey that is dark and more strongly flavored, you may want to reduce the amount to ⅓ cup.

# Diabetics' No Caraway Rye

2 pkg. active dry yeast
¼ cup lukewarm water
   (100 to 110°F)
1 cup lukewarm milk
1¾ cups lukewarm water
2½ tsp. salt
2 Tbs. molasses
2 Tbs. vegetable oil
2 cups whole-grain rye flour
2 Tbs. vital wheat gluten
3 to 3½ cups bread flour, divided

Optional Topping
egg white wash (one egg white
   + 1 Tbs. of water)
sesame seeds or poppy seeds
kosher salt

---

In a small bowl, dissolve yeast in warm water with a pinch of sugar, and allow to develop for 5 minutes or until foamy. Combine milk, water, salt, molasses, and oil in a medium mixing bowl. Place the yeast and the milk mixture in a large mixing bowl. Add rye flour and gluten, then beat 200 strokes.

Add 3 cups of bread flour, 1 cup at a time, mixing thoroughly after each addition. Turn dough out onto a lightly floured surface and knead for 3 minutes, adding small amounts of the remaining flour to keep the dough manageable. Cover the dough with a clean, dry dish towel and allow to rest for 5 minutes as the flours absorb the moisture. After the resting period, knead the dough for another 5 to 7 minutes. The resulting dough should be slightly sticky and firm but not stiff. Lightly oil the surface of the dough and place it in the rinsed mixing bowl. Cover with a towel and let rise in a warm, draft-free place for 60 to 90 minutes, or until doubled in bulk.

Punch the dough down and knead briefly to expel the larger air bubbles. Divide the dough and form into two oblong loaves. Place loaves on a lightly greased baking sheet. Cover and allow to rise until nearly doubled, 30 to 45 minutes.

Preheat oven to 375°F. If desired, gently brush the tops of the loaves with the egg white wash and sprinkle with seeds and a little salt. Bake for 30 to 40 minutes or until tops are medium brown and sound hollow when tapped. Cool on wire racks.

## NOTES:

— Finding healthy foods in the bread aisle can be a challenge for diabetics, so serve them this yummy rye bread. Studies have shown that rye bread has a more moderate effect on blood sugar, and the whole grain flour is high in fiber as well.

— Rye breads traditionally include caraway seeds, but I don't care much for that flavor, so I've omitted them here.

— If you want sandwich bread, I've also had success with this bread baked in lightly greased 8½ x 4½ x 2½ inch loaf pans. They may have to stay in the oven a bit longer depending upon the thickness of the pans—usually 45 to 50 minutes is about right. If you have trouble judging at first, use an instant read thermometer; the bread is done at an interior temperature of at least 195°F.

# Honey Mocha Bread

2 pkg. active dry yeast
1 cup lukewarm water
    (100 to 110°F)
½ cup honey
1 cup lukewarm milk
1 cup rye flour

¼ cup cocoa powder
1 Tbs. instant coffee
2 Tbs. vegetable oil
2 tsp. salt
4½ to 5 cups bread flour

---

    In a medium-size bowl, combine yeast with warm water and honey, and stir until completely dissolved—allow to stand for about 5 minutes. Add milk, rye flour, cocoa, coffee, oil, and salt; stir until thoroughly blended. Add 4 cups of flour, 1 cup at a time, mixing each time until the flour is completely incorporated. Turn dough out onto a lightly floured board and knead, adding small amounts of flour as needed to keep the dough manageable. Both the honey and the rye flour will keep the dough sticky, so be careful not to add too much flour—periodically, scrape up any dough sticking to the counter and knead it in. Knead for 10 to 12 minutes, until you have a slightly stiff dough. Rinse and dry the bowl, then oil the surface of the dough and place it in the bowl. Cover with a clean, dry dish towel, and let rise in a warm place free from drafts until doubled, about 60 to 75 minutes.

    Punch dough down and let rest for 5 minutes. Divide dough into 2 equal portions and form each piece into a fat oval. Place both loaves on a lightly greased baking sheet (you can also sprinkle a little cornmeal on the pan if you like that sort of bottom crust, or use parchment paper). Cover and let rise for 30 to 45 minutes (or until nearly doubled) in a warm place free from drafts. Bake in the lower third of a preheated 350°F oven for 30 to 35 minutes, or until the crust is dark brown and the loaf sounds hollow when tapped on the bottom. If the loaves seem to be darkening too quickly, cover them lightly with aluminum foil until the last 5 to 10 minutes of baking. Cool loaves on wire rack.

## NOTES:

— I'm a big fan of rye flour (I even add a little to my pizza dough on occasion), and I prefer honey over any other sweetener. So I developed this recipe for a bread that uses rye flour and honey, along with two other favorite flavors of mine, cocoa and coffee. The result is this dark loaf with a light texture that goes with just about any hearty meal, but especially well with beef dishes. The mocha flavor is quite subtle, so don't be expecting something like mocha almond fudge ice cream or gourmet coffee.

— You will almost certainly have to cover the loaves with foil for part of the baking time, as the honey in the dough makes them brown quickly. You can also bake these loaves in medium-size loaf pans (8½ x 4½ x 2½ inches), but I like these free-form loaves better. Since these flavors pair well with beef, consider shaping the dough into buns for hamburgers on the grill.

# Honey Corn Rolls

1 pkg. active dry yeast
1 cup lukewarm milk
1 egg, lightly beaten
¼ cup honey
1 tsp. salt

½ cup yellow cornmeal
2½ cups unbleached bread
    flour, divided
2 Tbs. vegetable oil

---

In a medium-size bowl, dissolve yeast in milk and allow to develop for about 5 minutes. Stir in egg, honey, salt, and cornmeal and mix well. Add 1½ cups of flour and beat until smooth. Add the oil and beat until it is fully incorporated. Add ¾ of a cup of the remaining flour and mix to form a dough that pulls away from the sides of the bowl.

Turn dough out onto a lightly floured board or countertop. Knead for 5 to 8 minutes, adding more flour as needed to make a smooth and elastic dough that is only slightly sticky. Lightly oil the surface of the dough and place in a clean, dry bowl. Cover with a dry cloth and let rise about an hour or until doubled in bulk.

Punch the dough down and knead it lightly to remove the larger air bubbles. Divide dough into 12 even pieces and shape into balls. Place balls into the cups of a lightly greased muffin tin. Cover and let rise for 30 minutes or until nearly doubled. Bake in a preheated 350°F oven for 15 to 20 minutes or until browned. The interior temperature of the rolls should be above 190°F. Remove from oven and allow to cool slightly before serving warm.

## NOTES:

— The cornmeal gives these rolls a little extra flavor and texture, and the use of the higher-protein bread flour makes them a bit chewier than most dinner rolls. They make a nice alternative to corn bread when served with ham and bean soup, chili, and hearty stews.

— I don't always have bread flour in the pantry, but I always keep gluten powder around. One teaspoon per cup of all-purpose flour adds the necessary protein to give these rolls their chewy character.

— My sister Anj sent me a version of this recipe years ago and I've tweaked it several times since then. Our Fr. Ronald says he wishes I would make these more often and more of them, since he likes them for breakfast as well!

— These rolls brown quickly because of the honey, so I don't recommend any egg wash or other glaze.

# Millet Bread

½ cup whole millet
½ cup rolled oats
2 cups boiling water
2 pkgs. active dry yeast
¼ cup lukewarm water
    (100 to 110°F)
⅓ cup honey

2 Tbs. olive oil
2 tsp. salt
grated zest of one medium orange
(optional) ½ cup shelled, toasted
    sunflower seeds (unsalted)
2 cups whole wheat flour
3 to 3½ cups all-purpose flour

---

In a medium-size bowl, combine millet and oats with hot water—stir until well blended and cool to lukewarm. Dissolve yeast in warm water and let stand for 10 minutes. Stir yeast and honey into millet mixture, followed by oil, salt, orange zest, and sunflower seeds (if desired). Add whole wheat flour and stir until flour is thoroughly incorporated. Repeat with 2 cups of all-purpose flour. Add remaining flour about ½ cup at a time until you have a soft dough.

Turn dough out onto a lightly floured board and knead for 8 to 10 minutes, adding small amounts of white flour as needed to keep dough manageable. The finished dough should be moderately soft and rather sticky. Lightly oil the surface of the dough and place it back into rinsed bowl and cover with a clean, dry towel. Allow to rise in a warm place free from drafts until doubled, 60 to 75 minutes.

Lightly grease a baking sheet. Punch dough down and knead briefly to expel larger air bubbles. Divide dough into 3 portions and shape each into a smooth ball. Place loaves on baking sheet. Cover loaves with a clean, dry cloth and allow to rise until nearly doubled, about 30 minutes.

Bake in a preheated 375°F oven for 20 to 25 minutes, or until browned on top and loaves sound hollow when tapped on the bottom; the interior temperature should be at least 195°F. Cool on racks.

**NOTES:**

— Millet is the oldest of the cultivated cereals: it consists of small, round, straw yellow grains, like tow-colored buckshot. Most people today consider millet, literally, for the birds; it's a primary ingredient in bird feed. But this grain was held in such high esteem in ancient times that it was called "Father Millet." I actually developed this bread for an article I wrote for Father's Day.

— I love the crunch that the whole millet provides here, which has a different density from the toasted sunflower seeds. The oatmeal changes the texture of the body of bread as well, so this recipe yields a "mouth feel" that is unique.

# Nine Grain Bread

## Sponge
1 cup lukewarm water
    (100 to 110°F)
2 pkg. active dry yeast
1 cup bread flour
½ cup whole wheat flour
1 tsp. brown sugar

## Dough
All of sponge
1½ cups warm water
2 Tbs. brown sugar
2 Tbs. vegetable oil
2 tsp. salt
1 cup nine-grain cereal mix
¼ cup flaxseed
¼ cup millet
4¼ to 5 cups of bread flour

In a medium-size bowl, combine all of the ingredients for the sponge and beat until smooth. Allow the batter to sit for 20 minutes, or until foamy and doubled in volume. Add the remaining water, brown sugar, oil, and salt, and beat until smooth. Add cereal mix, flaxseed, and millet, and stir until thoroughly incorporated. Add 2 cups of flour and beat until thoroughly incorporated. Repeat with 2 more cups of flour. About ¼ cup at a time, work in enough of remaining flour to form a soft dough—it will be quite sticky, but resist the temptation to add too much more flour. Turn dough out onto a lightly floured surface and knead for 10 to 12 minutes. Rinse and dry the bowl, then oil the surface of the dough and place in the bowl. Cover with a clean, dry dish towel, and let rise in a warm place free from drafts for about 1 hour, or until doubled in volume. Punch dough down and knead briefly to expel larger air bubbles. Form into loaves and place in lightly greased 9 × 5 × 3 inch loaf pans. Cover with a clean, dry dish towel and allow to rise until doubled, about 45 minutes. Bake in a preheated 375°F oven for 40 to 45 minutes. Loaves should be golden brown, slide easily from the pan, and sound hollow when tapped on the bottom. Cool on wire racks.

**NOTES:**

— The nine-grain cereal used for this bread is not the kind that you pour milk over, it's used to make hot cereal, like oatmeal or porridge. You can usually find it in the bulk-foods section of a large supermarket or health food store, and it may be a blend of five or seven grains instead of nine. Whatever you find will work just dandy.

— This bread is among the all-time Saint Bede Abbey favorites—my fellow monks devour it whenever it is served! It makes excellent toast at breakfast, serves as a hearty base for a sandwich of lunchmeat and cheese, and goes well with just about any dinner entree. Fr. Patrick in particular loves this bread and will go to the kitchen before supper to hunt down the slices remaining from lunch and take them to his place at table. I sit at the same table and I'm pleased to report that he always shares the wealth!

— I developed this recipe for Mike the Deli Guy, to use as a base for the turkey sandwich at his shop. He would come over once a week or so and we'd bake about 16 loaves: 12 for him, 4 for the monks. The original recipe begins with "Pour 20 cups of warm water into the 50 quart bowl of the Hobart mixer."

# No-Knead Oatmeal Rolls

1 cup boiling water
1½ cups rolled oats
2 pkg. active dry yeast
½ cup lukewarm water
    (100 to 110°F)
2 cups lukewarm milk

½ cup sugar
1 Tbs. salt
5 cups all-purpose flour
½ cup (1 stick) butter, melted
extra oatmeal for topping
    (optional)

In a large bowl, pour boiling water over oats and stir thoroughly. Allow to cool to lukewarm (about 30 minutes). In a small bowl, combine yeast with warm water and stir until dissolved. Allow to sit for 5 minutes. Add yeast and milk to oatmeal and stir until blended. Stir in sugar and salt. Add flour, 1 cup at a time, beating vigorously until each cup is thoroughly incorporated into the batter. Lastly, add the melted butter and beat well until batter is smooth. Cover the rinsed bowl with a towel and let rise in a warm place, free from drafts, until doubled (about 30 to 45 minutes). Stir batter down and beat vigorously for about 2 minutes. Lightly grease muffin tins. Pour ¼ cup of batter into each cup and sprinkle with oatmeal if desired. Allow batter to rise to the top of each cup, about 15 minutes. Bake in a preheated 400°F oven about 25 minutes or until browned on top. Remove rolls from pans and cool slightly on wire racks—serve warm. Makes 30 rolls.

## NOTES:

— One year the day before Thanksgiving I made a huge batch of oatmeal roll dough in our giant Hobart mixer, and I had five grade school kids over from a local parish to make rolls for their Thanksgiving dinner. We had great fun forming the dough into different shapes: bowknots, fantans, cloverleafs, etc. They all left with homemade rolls for their families, and I had enough to feed the monks and over 30 friends and family who joined us for our Thanksgiving meal. This recipe is a streamlined version of those rolls, formed as a thick batter instead of a kneaded dough.

— It really is important to stir the batter vigorously after the first rising, to redistribute the yeast to make for an even texture in the roll. The outer crust of these rolls is thick and chewy because of the oatmeal, but the interior remains soft and fluffy.

— A batch of 30 rolls may seem like a lot, but if you have the whole family over for Thanksgiving, you may need that many. If not, pop a dozen or so into the freezer for that upcoming Christmas office party or Boy Scout potluck. If you don't have enough muffin tins or oven space to make all 30 rolls at once, you can divide the batter in half and refrigerate one portion while the first batch bakes. Then let the batter come to room temperature, stir it down again, and fill the muffin tins again for a second bake.

# Pumpernickel

½ cup bread crumbs,
    toasted dark
⅓ cup cornmeal
2 cups hot water
¼ cup lukewarm water
    (100 to 110°F)
1 tsp. brown sugar
2 pkg. active dry yeast
¼ cup molasses

¼ cup oil
2 Tbs. cider vinegar
1 egg
1 Tbs. salt
2 Tbs. gluten powder
1 Tbs. cocoa powder
2 Tbs. instant coffee granules
3½ cups rye flour
2 to 2½ cups bread flour

---

Place bread crumbs, cornmeal, and hot water in a large mixing bowl and mix thoroughly. Cool to lukewarm (100 to 110°F). In the meantime, place ¼ cup warm water, brown sugar, and yeast in a small bowl and stir to dissolve. Allow yeast to develop for 10 minutes. Add molasses, oil, vinegar, egg, and salt to cornmeal mixture and stir with a heavy wooden spoon until blended. Stir in yeast, gluten, cocoa powder, and coffee granules, along with 2 cups of rye flour. Allow to rest for 5 minutes.

Add remaining rye flour and stir until flour is thoroughly incorporated. Add 1 cup bread flour, mixing the dough with your hands—the dough will seem very sticky and won't hold together very well, but be patient. Turn dough out onto a well-floured board and knead for 12 to 15 minutes, adding small amounts of bread flour to keep the dough manageable. The finished dough will be sticky, slightly elastic, and very stiff. Oil surface of the dough and place in the rinsed bowl; cover with a clean, dry cloth and allow to rise until doubled (60 to 75 minutes) in a warm place free from drafts.

Punch dough down and knead for about a minute. Form into a large round loaf or 2 oblong loaves and place on a lightly greased baking sheet (you may also use baking parchment). Cover and let rise until nearly doubled, about 45 minutes. Bake in a preheated oven at 375°F for 55 to 60 minutes, or until crust is hard and loaves sound hollow when tapped. They will not sound as hollow as other breads because pumpernickel is a rather dense bread. The interior temperature of the bread should be about 200°F. Cool on racks. Slice thin to serve.

## NOTES:

— This is not a bread for the faint of heart! The dough is very sticky and heavy and requires a lot of kneading. But if you prefer hearty, dense pumpernickel to the fluff found in most grocery stores, you'll be glad you made the effort. Many of my confreres of German or Polish background were delighted when I started experimenting with pumpernickel. My first few attempts at pumpernickel were incredibly dense and heavy, but the brethren gamely ate 3 loaves of failure before I got to this success! They were surprised to discover, as I was, that this bread has so many unusual ingredients. Legend has it that it was originally developed during a shortage of white flour, so other dry ingredients were added as extenders. It is not as dark as many commercial pumpernickels, which are almost always artificially colored.

— Some recipes add mashed potatoes to pumpernickel dough, but I find that makes the dough a little too dense. The use of toasted bread crumbs adds to the unique texture. Toast finely ground bread crumbs by spreading them on a cookie sheet and baking at 350°F for 15 to 20 minutes, or until they are slightly darker than graham crackers. Be careful not to let them burn. You can use white, whole wheat, or rye breads for your crumbs. If you use leftover pumpernickel, your bread will be correspondingly darker.

— Because this bread is so dense, it doesn't toast very well. Be sure to slice it thin, whether for a sandwich or as an accompaniment to a meal. Try it for a deli meat sandwich, or with a strong Havarti cheese and cold beer.

# Seeded Barley Bread

## Sponge

1½ cups lukewarm water
    (100 to 110°F)
1½ cups barley flour
½ cup whole wheat flour
1 pkg. active dry yeast

(Mix ingredients thoroughly in a
non-metallic bowl and cover with
a towel. Allow to ferment in a
warm place free from drafts for
2 to 6 hours.)

## Dough

All of sponge, torn into pieces
1 cup lukewarm milk
    (100 to 110°F)
2 tsp. salt
2 Tbs. gluten powder
¼ cup vegetable oil
¼ cup molasses
⅓ cup unsalted sunflower
    kernels, coarsely chopped
3 Tbs. flaxseed meal
3 to 3½ cups bread flour

Prepare sponge in a large non-metallic bowl 2 to 6 hours before baking. Add to the sponge the warm milk, salt, gluten, oil, and molasses and beat until smooth. Allow to develop for 30 minutes. Add the seeds along with 2 cups of the bread flour and stir until well blended. Add the remaining flour about half a cup at a time, each time mixing thoroughly until the flour is completely incorporated into the dough, until you have a slightly sticky dough that is firm enough to knead. Turn dough out onto a lightly floured board and knead for 8 minutes, adding small amounts of flour as needed to keep dough manageable. At the end of the kneading period, dough should be somewhat soft rather than stiff, but only slightly sticky. Oil the surface of the dough and place back in the rinsed bowl. Cover with a towel and allow to rise at room temperature for 60 to 90 minutes, or until doubled. Punch dough down and knead briefly to work out the larger air bubbles. Dough may be formed into 1 large or 2 medium free-form loaves and placed on a lightly greased baking sheet, or divided into 2 and placed in standard loaf pans. Cover and let rise for 30 to 45 minutes or until nearly doubled. Bake in a preheated 375°F oven for 35 to 45 minutes, until crust is brown and loaf sounds hollow when tapped. Cool on racks.

**NOTES:**

— Our Fr. James of happy memory eagerly devoured whole wheat and pumpernickel, as well as this barley bread. His love for this particular bread was illustrated when I made a large round loaf of Seeded Barley Bread late one night, intending to serve it at lunch the next day. After morning prayer I wandered out into the kitchen with my cup of coffee, only to discover that a huge slab had already been cut from the loaf, evidently well before breakfast! Knowing Fr. James's propensity for early rising, I knew immediately who the culprit was. But how can you scold someone who so obviously appreciates your efforts?

— This bread could be considered among the popular "artisan" breads, which are characterized by a long, slow rising period with a relatively small amount of yeast, sometimes as little as 1 teaspoon. Slow-rise breads have more flavor, so avoid the temptation to add more yeast, or to speed up the process by adding sugar to the sponge.

— Barley is one of the earliest cultivated grains and was commonly used for bread in biblical times. It makes a mild flour that is somewhat sweeter than wheat, sometimes even imparting a slightly nutty flavor to breads. In this loaf, however, the long rising period for the sponge adds a slight tang as well, resulting in a loaf of complex flavors and textures.

— If you can find mini-sunflower seeds, there is no need to chop them. Their flavor becomes more pronounced when this bread is toasted.

# Ethnic Breads

# Austrian Povitica

| | |
|---|---|
| 1 batch of basic dough, white (see page 8) or wheat (see page 6) | 1½ to 2 lbs. bacon<br>1 lb. chopped walnuts<br>2 Tbs. sugar<br>6 eggs |

Follow instructions for any simple white bread recipe up to the first rising. While it is rising, chop uncooked bacon into small pieces and fry until cooked, but not crisp. Drain and set aside. After dough has doubled, punch down dough and knead for 3 minutes to work out the air bubbles—allow dough to relax for 5 or 10 minutes, which will make it easier to roll out. Roll out onto a large lightly floured counter or pastry cloth to 24 by 20 inches, about ¼ inch thick. Spread bacon bits and walnuts evenly over dough, then sprinkle the sugar on top, followed by the walnuts. Beat the eggs thoroughly and pour over filling and dough.

Roll up the dough lengthwise jellyroll style. Pull slightly on the dough to get a tight roll, but be careful not to tear holes in the dough. Seal the edges, then coil into an oval loaf with the two edges tucked into the center (see photo). Place in a lightly greased 9 × 13 × 2½ inch loaf pan. Cover with a clean cloth and let rise in a warm place until doubled in bulk, about 50 minutes.

Preheat oven to 450°F. If any of the egg mixture has leaked out during rising, brush this over the top of the loaf for a glaze. (In any case, get as much of the egg out of the bottom of the pan as possible, or it will cause the bottom crust to burn.) Bake for 10 minutes at 450°F, then reduce heat to 350°F and bake for about 40 minutes, or until nicely browned. If the bread begins to brown too much on top, cover the loaf lightly with aluminum foil until the last 10 minutes of baking. If your oven doesn't bake evenly, turn the pan around at least once during the baking process to ensure the bread is being baked thoroughly on all sides. Remove from oven and let cool in pan for 15 minutes before transferring to a wire rack to cool completely.

**NOTES:**

— This recipe has been in my family for four generations. My great-grandmother, Frances Zunic Sardick, brought it to this country from Austria. You often see Croatian or Slovenian versions of this bread (usually called potica), which use ground walnuts, cream, honey, and a much sweeter dough rolled into very thin layers. They are very popular at Christmas in our area, but I find them too dry and a bit dull compared to this beauty, which bakes up as a large, dramatic loaf with exquisite flavors and textures.

— Povitica is a traditional holiday bread, and in my family a special treat for Easter, at the end of Lenten fasts and meatless meals. When my mother was a little girl, my grandmother used to make it on Good Friday to serve Saturday night. How she could stand to fry bacon and bake bread on the most important day of fast and abstinence in the church calendar, I can't imagine! She was certainly made of sterner stuff than Mom and Grandpa Frankie, who would leave the house and visit every church in a 25-mile radius to escape the tempting aromas.

# Barm Brack

2 pkg. active dry yeast
2 cups strong black tea, divided
    and cooled to lukewarm
½ cup brown sugar
1½ cup raisins
2 eggs, lightly beaten

¼ cup (½ stick) butter, melted
1½ tsp. salt
1 to 2 tsp. of mixed spice
    (see note)
6¼ to 6¾ cups all-purpose flour

In a small bowl, dissolve yeast and a pinch of brown sugar in ¼ cup of tea; allow to develop. In a medium-size bowl, dissolve brown sugar in the remaining 1¾ cups of tea; add raisins and allow to soak for 10 minutes. Add yeast mixture to tea. Stir in eggs, butter, salt, and spices. Stir in 6 cups of flour, 1 cup at a time, mixing after each addition until flour is completely incorporated.

You can use any number of spices for this traditional Irish bread, including nutmeg, ginger, cinnamon, cloves, allspice, anise, and mace. My favorite: 1 teaspoon of cinnamon, ¼ teaspoon each of nutmeg and mace, with a pinch of ground anise seed.

Turn dough out onto a lightly floured board and knead for 6 to 8 minutes, adding small amounts of flour as needed to keep dough manageable. The finished dough should be moderately soft and only slightly sticky. Lightly oil the surface of the dough and place it back into the rinsed bowl and cover with a clean, dry towel. Allow to rise in a warm place free from drafts until doubled, 60 to 75 minutes.

Lightly grease three 9-inch pie pans. Punch dough down and knead briefly to expel larger air bubbles. Divide dough into 3 portions and shape each into a flattened round about 8 inches across. Place loaves in pie plates. Cover loaves with a clean, dry cloth and allow to rise until nearly doubled, about 30 minutes.

Bake in a preheated 375°F oven for 20 to 25 minutes, or until browned on top and loaves sound hollow when tapped on the bottom. Cool on racks.

## NOTES:

— This fragrant loaf is traditionally served on Halloween with a gold ring or other charm baked into it that is supposed to bring luck to the person who received it. I like to serve it all year long, minus the good luck piece. I figure that if the brethren are getting homemade bread, they're lucky enough!

—There is some disagreement as to the meaning of the name "barm brack." It could mean "bread made from barm" (a yeasty by-product of beer making) or it may be a corruption of the Anglo-Irish *bairigen breac*, meaning "speckled cake." Most recipes for barm brack yield only a single loaf, but I figure everyone knows someone of Irish ancestry who would appreciate getting a tasty gift. You can also bake this bread in two 8½ x 4½ x 2½ inch loaf pans, but you'll need to bake them for 40 to 45 minutes. I like the rounded form better, since it looks more rustic, an effect that is increased by slashing a cross in the top of each loaf just before it goes into the oven.

# Brioche

1 pkg. active dry yeast
1 cup lukewarm whole milk (100
    to 110°F)
¼ cup sugar
4½ cups all-purpose flour,
    divided
4 eggs

1 egg yolk (reserve white for
    egg wash)
1¼ tsp. salt
½ cup (1 stick) of butter,
    softened
egg wash (1 egg white beaten
    with 1 Tbs. of water)
sugar for sprinkling

---

Dissolve yeast in warmed milk, then stir in sugar along with 1 cup of flour. Allow to sit for 15 minutes for yeast to develop. Add eggs, egg yolk, and salt, then beat well. Add 3 cups of the remaining flour, 1 cup at a time, stirring thoroughly each time. The dough at this point will be a very stiff batter, quite sticky. Turn the dough out onto a smooth surface (marble is ideal) and stretch and fold the batter over itself to develop the gluten network. Continue for 8 to 10 minutes, keeping hands lightly dusted with flour to keep the dough manageable—I actually keep one hand dusted with flour and hold a bench knife, dough scraper, or spatula in the other to manipulate the dough. The dough will eventually become more cohesive, although still sticky. Coat the surface of the dough with oil or butter and place back in the rinsed bowl. Cover with a towel and allow to rise for 60 to 90 minutes, or until doubled.

Punch dough down, then knead in the butter about 2 tablespoons at a time, working quickly. There may be some small bits of butter visible which are not entirely incorporated, but that's OK. Place dough back in bowl, cover with a damp towel, and refrigerate for at least 2 hours or overnight (this helps the dough firm up and become easier to shape). Lightly grease a large brioche pan (you can also use a 2-quart round pan or casserole dish). Punch dough down and knead briefly to expel air. Divide off ¼ of the dough. Form the larger portion into a round ball and place in the pan. Form the smaller piece into a ball, make an indentation in the top of the larger piece, and place the smaller ball on top. Cover and let rise until nearly doubled, 30 to 45 minutes. Preheat oven to 350°F. Gently brush the top of the risen loaf with egg wash and sprinkle with sugar. Place pan in the lower third of the oven and bake for 50 to 60 minutes, or until bread is golden to dark brown. Remove from oven and allow to sit for about 30 minutes before removing loaf from pan (this helps the loaf firm up and keeps it from collapsing once it is removed from the pan). Cool on a wire rack.

For small brioches

After dough has been refrigerated and punched down, divide dough into 12 portions. Separate a piece about the size of a large olive from each portion, rolling each into a ball. Place larger portions in lightly greased brioche pans or muffin tins, make an indentation in each, and place smaller balls on top. Let rise, brush with egg wash, and sprinkle with sugar. Bake at 350°F for 15 to 20 minutes, or until tops are golden brown. Remove from pans and cool on wire racks.

## notes:

— Many recipes for brioche have been simplified to make them more like your usual bread dough recipe. My version is more traditional than most. The first time you make brioche, you may be put off by how soft and sticky the dough is, but don't fret. Once you've worked the butter in and it has been refrigerated, the dough is pretty easy to work with. The hardest part is getting the little topknot to stay in the center of the loaf while it rises. Mine often slide off to one side, giving the brioche a slightly drunken appearance!

— My confreres at St. Bede enjoy having small brioches for breakfast, which are exquisite with unsalted butter and apricot preserves.

— You can use this dough to make brioche donuts, which are the absolute pinnacle of breakfast breads, in my opinion. Incredibly rich and quite addictive, they are the culinary equivalent of mortal sin in butter cream frosting. I got the idea for using brioche dough for donuts from *Blue Ribbon Breads* by Mary Ward and Carol Stine.

# Challah

### Sponge
2 pkg. active dry yeast
1 Tbs. granulated sugar
1 cup lukewarm water
   (100 to 110°F)
2 cups bread flour

### Dough
all of sponge
1½ cups water
¾ cup vegetable oil

3 eggs
1 Tbs. salt
1 tsp. cinnamon
1 Tbs. vanilla extract
½ cup sugar
4 to 5½ cups of bread flour
1 egg beaten with 1 Tbs. water
   (to brush the top)
sesame seeds or poppy seeds
   (optional)

---

Start by making the sponge. In a small bowl, dissolve yeast and sugar in the water. Add 2 cups of the flour and let stand for 30 to 60 minutes to allow the yeast to develop. For the dough, combine water, oil, and eggs in a large bowl and mix well. Stir in the salt, cinnamon, vanilla, and sugar. Add the yeast sponge and beat until smooth. Add the remaining flour, about a cup at a time, until you get slightly firm dough—it will be a bit softer than ordinary bread dough because of the eggs. Knead for about 5 minutes, and then let rise, covered, about an hour and a half or until doubled in bulk.

Punch down the dough and turn it out onto a lightly floured surface. Knead briefly to work out the larger air pockets. Divide the dough into seven equal pieces and roll each piece into a rope about 12 inches long. Braid four of these ropes together, tucking the ends underneath. Place on a lightly greased baking sheet. Braid the remaining three ropes and gently place them on top of the four-rope braid. Cover with a towel and let rise until nearly doubled in bulk—the loaf will be quite large.

Brush all over with the beaten egg and sprinkle with sesame or poppy seed if desired. Bake in preheated oven at 375°F until golden brown, about 45 minutes. If your oven doesn't bake evenly, be sure to turn the pan around every 15 minutes or so. Cool on a rack.

**NOTES:**

— I've seen many different recipes for challah, but I like Marian Honig's version (found in her excellent book *Breads of the World*), which I have adapted here. Her addition of small amounts of vanilla and cinnamon make this bread smell heavenly as it's baking. This recipe takes a lot of time and effort, but it's really worth it. The large braided loaf is the traditional form, but you can make two smaller single braids, or form wreaths.

— There are many Jewish traditions regarding this "queen of breads," including specific prayers to be said as it is made and when it is eaten. Don't be hesitant to contact a local synagogue for resources to learn more, especially if one of those resources is a Jewish grandmother willing to give you a lesson or two!

# Ciabatta

## Starter
1 tsp. of active dry yeast (save
    the rest of the package
    for later)
¾ cup lukewarm water
    (100 to 110°F)
1 cup bread flour
pinch of sugar

## Dough
1 cup lukewarm water
remainder of package of yeast
    (about 1¼ tsp.)
1 tsp. salt
1 Tbs. olive oil
1 tsp. honey
2½ cups bread flour

Make starter 6 to 12 hours ahead. Pour ¾ cup of warm water into a large, non-metallic bowl and sprinkle 1 teaspoon of yeast on top (be sure to save the remainder of the yeast for later). Stir to dissolve, then add flour and sugar and beat until smooth. Cover with plastic wrap and leave in a warm place for 6 to 12 hours.

Dissolve the remainder of the package of yeast in one cup of warm water and add to starter with salt, oil, and honey. Beat mixture until smooth. Add remaining 2½ cups of flour (it's OK to add it all at once) and mix until thoroughly incorporated. The dough will be halfway between a batter and regular bread dough—hard to stir but too wet to knead. Let mixture rest for about 5 minutes, then beat and fold dough with a heavy wooden spoon, plastic dough scraper, or heavy-duty rubber spatula for 5 minutes. Divide dough in half and place in heavily oiled bowls or serving platters. Cover with oiled plastic wrap and let rise for 1½ to 2 hours, until nearly tripled in bulk. Prepare a heavily floured baking sheet, and have extra flour to dust your hands. Turn one dough out onto the baking sheet very carefully, without deflating the air bubbles, and run your fingers along the side to plump the loaf and form the distinctive "slipper" shape. Repeat with second loaf. Let rise, uncovered, for another 30 minutes. Bake in preheated 400°F oven for 30 to 35 minutes, 40 minutes if you prefer a crisper crust. Remove from pans and let cool on racks. This bread is best eaten on the day it is made, but if you must store it, use a waxed paper bag from the bakery rather than plastic, to keep the crust crisp.

## NOTES:

— The word *ciabatta* means "slipper," as this bread often takes that oblong shape. The dough is supposed to be very slack, having a high liquid content, so don't add more flour to make the dough more manageable. The wet dough produces a delightfully thin, crisp crust, and the long rising periods make the interior very soft, with large holes. Fr. Ronald says ciabatta reminds him of the breads they served at Sant'Anselmo in Rome.

— You really do have to have bread flour for this recipe to turn out well. Bread flour is milled from harder wheat with a higher gluten content, so it can stand up to the long fermentation process and keep its shape even in such a slack dough.

— I've seen a rather squarish ciabatta used for a grilled eggplant sandwich at the Pearl Bakery in Portland, Oregon—their backroom bakers showed me how to handle ciabatta dough carefully to keep the air bubbles intact, which is essential to the airy interior texture.

# Cuban Bread

3 pkg. active dry yeast
4 tsp. brown sugar
2 cups lukewarm water
   (100 to 110°F)

5 to 6 cups bread flour,
   divided
1 Tbs. salt
egg wash (egg white or whole
   egg mixed with 1 Tbs. water)

---

In a medium-size bowl, combine yeast, sugar, and water and stir until dissolved. Add 2 cups of flour and beat well. Allow to develop for 10 minutes, then stir in salt. Add remaining flour, about a cup at a time, until a stiff dough forms. Turn out onto a lightly floured board and knead for 8 to 10 minutes, adding more flour as needed to keep dough manageable. Dough should be smooth, elastic, and not sticky. Oil the surface of the dough and place in the rinsed bowl; cover and let rise until doubled in bulk, 45 to 60 minutes. Punch the dough down, knead lightly, and form into long loaves. Place loaves on a baking sheet sprinkled with cornmeal. Let rise, uncovered, for 10 minutes. Using a sharp knife or razor blade, slash the tops of the loaves diagonally 3 or 4 times. Brush the loaves with the egg wash and place on the middle shelf of a COLD oven. On the bottom shelf, place a shallow pan into which ¾ cup of hot water has been poured. Turn oven on to 400°F and bake for 35 to 40 minutes or until well browned and loaves sound hollow when tapped. Cool on racks.

## nOTES:

— I have seen several different versions of Cuban bread, including one that calls for 4 tablespoons of yeast (nearly 5 packages), which seems to me a little excessive. But they all have a few things in common: extra yeast, a large proportion of salt, a cold oven to start, and a pan of hot water to help develop the crust.

— This is one of the few recipes that I would say really requires bread flour to be its best. All-purpose flour works OK but often produces a low loaf if not kneaded thoroughly.

— One recipe I tested suggested brushing the loaves with cold water before they went into the oven. I did so, as gently as I could—and the loaves deflated, never to rise again. The taste was fine, but the loaves lacked the open-holed texture which characterizes "pan de cubana." I also discovered that ¾ cup of hot water in the bottom of the oven was just enough to achieve the perfect crust—most recipes don't specify the amount of water.

— Notice the absence of oil or butter in the dough, which makes the bread crustier but also means that it won't keep long. But this bread is so good you won't have to worry much about leftovers. If you think you'll only use one loaf within a day, don't freeze the other—just give it away!

— This bread is outstanding as a base for quick broiler pizzas. Cut the loaf lengthwise, brush on pizza sauce and add toppings, then warm under the broiler until the cheese starts to brown slightly. The crisp crust makes a delightful crunch as you bite into it. I also like Cuban bread as a base for sub sandwiches.

# French Baguettes

1 pkg. active dry yeast
2½ cups lukewarm water
   (100 to 110°F)
3 cups bread flour

2 tsp. salt
3 to 3½ cups all-purpose flour
cornmeal for sprinkling
1 egg white (optional)

---

In a large bowl, dissolve yeast in warm water. Add salt and bread flour and beat until smooth. Cover bowl with plastic wrap and let yeast develop for 3 hours—batter will triple in volume and then begin to fall. Uncover and stir down batter. Add 3 cups all-purpose flour, 1 cup at a time, each time stirring until flour is thoroughly incorporated. Turn dough out onto a lightly floured surface and knead for 8 to 10 minutes, adding small amounts of flour as needed. The dough should be manageable, but still soft and rather moist. Oil the surface of the dough and place it in a clean bowl. Cover and let rise until doubled, about 1 hour.

Punch dough down and knead briefly. Divide dough into 3 portions, and roll each piece into an oval about 5 × 12 inches. Brush any excess flour off the top of the oval. Starting at the long end, roll each into a cylinder—as you roll, pull the dough slightly to stretch it tight, so there are no air pockets. Pinch to seal the seam (if necessary, brush the edges with water first). Lightly grease a 12 × 18 inch jellyroll pan and sprinkle lightly with cornmeal. Space loaves evenly, seam side down, on baking sheet and cover with a clean, dry towel. Let rise until doubled, 30 to 45 minutes.

About half an hour before baking, preheat oven to 450°F. On the bottom shelf, place a shallow pan with ¾ cup of water. If desired, mix egg white with 2 tablespoons water and brush tops of loaves. With a sharp knife or razor blade, slash the top of loaves with long diagonal cuts. Bake for 25 to 30 minutes (the breads could come out after as little as 20 minutes, but the longer baking time makes for a sturdier crust). Remove from pans and cool on wire racks. Best if served the same day as they are baked.

## NOTES:

— As many viewers know, French baguettes were my first bread baking project, back in fifth grade. I've learned how to bake hundreds of different breads since then, but I continue to return to this old favorite. My fellow monks love this bread as much as my grade-school classmates. Once I made 6 large baguettes for supper, and there was a bread bag filled with leftover slices. Fr. Philip came up into the kitchen that evening looking for a snack, and took the leftovers back to the TV room with some white cheddar cheese. He and Fr. Ambrose polished off the entire bag during the course of a Cubs—White Sox baseball game!

— The bread flour used at the beginning is able to stand up to the long process of a 3-hour fermentation, and the all-purpose flour added later on makes for a softer interior. But if you have only one kind of flour in the house, make the loaves anyway.

— Many baguette recipes recommend a 60-minute final proof, but every time I've let the loaves rise that long, they completely deflated when I slashed the tops, and the resulting loaves weren't as light as I had hoped. But if your kitchen is air conditioned, you may need that long, so experiment with different rising times—it's bread, it's going to forgive you!

# Hungarian Potato Bread

## Sponge
1 cup lukewarm water
    (100 to 110°F)
2 pkg. active dry yeast
1 tsp. honey
1 cup bread flour

## Dough
All of sponge
1 cup lukewarm water
2 Tbs. honey
1½ tsp. salt
1 to 1½ cups mashed potatoes
1 Tbs. anise, fennel, or caraway
    seeds (optional)
6 to 8 cups of flour

In a medium-size bowl, combine all the ingredients for the sponge and beat until smooth. Allow the batter to sit for 20 minutes, or until foamy and doubled in volume. Add the remaining cup of water, honey, salt, potatoes, and seeds (if desired) and beat until smooth. Add 2 cups of flour and beat until thoroughly incorporated. Repeat with 2 more cups of flour. About 1 cup at a time, work in enough of remaining flour to form a soft dough—the amount of flour will vary according to the amount of mashed potatoes you used. Turn dough out onto a lightly floured surface and knead for 8 to 10 minutes. Rinse and dry the bowl, then oil the surface of the dough and place in the bowl. Cover with a clean, dry dish towel, and let rise in a warm place free from drafts for about 1 hour, or until doubled in bulk.

Punch dough down and knead briefly to expel larger air bubbles. Form into loaves and place in lightly greased 9 × 5 × 3 inch loaf pans. Cover with a clean, dry dish towel and allow to rise until doubled, about 30 minutes. Brush the tops of the loaves with milk and sprinkle with more seeds, if desired. Bake in a preheated 375°F oven for 40 to 45 minutes. Loaves should be golden brown, slide easily from the pan, and sound hollow when tapped on the bottom. Cool on wire racks.

**NOTES:**

— I hate seeing food going to waste, and a lot of my baking is inspired by leftovers. If creamed corn appears at supper, I'll probably make cornmeal muffins for breakfast. Leftover ham or bacon gets chopped up for pizza topping. This Hungarian Potato Bread uses leftover mashed potatoes, and the size of the loaves will be determined in part by the amount of mashed potatoes you have on hand. The recipe as it stands will make two large 2-pound loaves. If you end up with a smaller amount of dough, use smaller pans. The truly traditional method would be to bake them free-form on baking stones or a lightly greased baking sheet.

— I developed the recipe on the assumption that the mashed potatoes would contain a certain amount of salt and butter or margarine. If you never have leftover mashed potatoes, peel and dice 2 medium-size potatoes and place them in a small saucepan in enough water to cover. Boil until soft, then drain (reserve the water to use for the recipe), and then mash them. You'll also want to increase the salt to 2 teaspoons, and add 2 tablespoons of butter with the potatoes.

— Although using fennel or caraway seeds is traditional, I prefer this bread without any seasoning—then you can really taste the difference the potatoes make.

# Pan de Muertos

## Starter
1 pkg. active dry yeast
1/4 cup lukewarm water
    (100 to 110°F)
1/2 cup all-purpose flour
1 egg

## Dough
all of starter
4 eggs, well beaten (reserve one
    yolk)

1/2 tsp. salt
1/3 cup sugar
1/2 cup butter, melted
zest and juice of one medium
    orange
4 1/2 cups all-purpose flour

## Topping
melted butter and granulated
    sugar

---

Make starter in a small bowl by dissolving yeast in warm water and allowing to sit for 10 minutes, then blending in egg and flour. Cover and let develop for 30 to 60 minutes. In a large bowl, combine starter with eggs (you may need to use an egg beater to get it smooth). Add salt, sugar, butter, juice, and zest, and mix well. Add 3 cups of flour, 1 cup at a time, mixing thoroughly each time. Add remaining flour about 1/4 cup at a time, until a soft dough is formed that pulls away from the sides of the bowl. Turn out onto a lightly floured board and knead for 5 minutes, adding small amounts of flour as needed to keep dough manageable. When finished, the dough should be soft but should spring back when pushed. Oil the surface of the dough lightly and place back in the rinsed bowl. Cover with a towel and let rise for 60 to 90 minutes, or until doubled.

Punch dough down, and set apart 1/4 of the dough. With the larger portion, form a low, round loaf, about 2 inches thick, and place it on a lightly greased baking sheet. Divide the remaining dough into 5 equal portions. Use one to form a smooth ball, and place it in the center of the loaf (this is meant to suggest a skull). Divide each remaining portion into 2, and roll them into rods about 4 inches long. Flatten the ends slightly (these are the bones). Place the bones in a circle radiating out from the skull (like spokes on a wheel), or arrange them in 4 crosses equally spaced around the center. Brush the bottom of each bone with a little water if you have trouble getting it to stick

to the loaf. Cover and let rise for 30 to 45 minutes, or until nearly doubled. Preheat oven to 350°F. Beat the remaining egg yolk with a tablespoon of water and brush the egg wash all over the loaf. Bake in the lower third of the oven for 35 to 40 minutes, or until it is golden brown and sounds hollow when tapped on the bottom. Remove from oven and cool on a rack for 30 minutes. Then brush loaf with melted butter and sprinkle generously with sugar.

## NOTES:

— This bread is a traditional part of All Saints' and All Souls' Day celebrations in Mexico. There are dozens of variations for this bread, which is taken to the cemetery along with other foods and flowers for a symbolic meal with those who are buried there. Not a morbid or sorrowful affair, the Day of the Dead is a time for celebrating the memory of beloved family members with special treats like this bread. Pan de Muertos has a cake-like quality to it and is delicious all by itself, without butter or other toppings.

— You can use the dough to form 2 to 4 smaller loaves as well. In some parts of Mexico, the bread comes in the shapes of people or animals.

— When I was testing this recipe, I took a batch to one of the Spanish classes in the Academy. I saw one of the students later that day, and she confided to me that "someone brought that 'dead bread' last year, but yours was lots better!"

# Red Onion Focaccia

## Dough

1 pkg. active dry yeast
1 cup lukewarm water
    (100 to 110°F)
1 Tbs. olive oil
1 tsp. salt
3 to 3½ cups all-purpose flour

## Topping

1 small red onion
3 Tbs. olive oil
olive oil and coarse salt

---

In a medium-size bowl, add yeast to warm water and stir to dissolve. Add salt and oil. Add 1 cup of flour and beat until smooth. Repeat with second cup of flour. A ¼ cup at a time, work in enough of remaining flour to form a soft dough. Knead for 6 to 8 minutes. Rinse and dry the bowl, then lightly oil the surface of the dough and place in the bowl. Cover with a clean, dry dish towel, and let rise in a warm place free from drafts for about 1 hour, or until doubled in volume. Punch dough down. On a lightly floured surface, pat or roll dough out into a circle 8 or 9 inches across. Place on a wooden peel or paddle which has been well-sprinkled with cornmeal. Cover and let rise for 20 minutes. Place a pizza stone on the middle shelf of the oven and preheat oven to 400°F. (Stone needs to preheat for at least 30 minutes.) Thinly slice the onion and toss with 3 tablespoons of olive oil. Dimple the surface of the dough with a fingertip, with holes about 1 inch apart. Lightly brush the surface of the dough with olive oil. Spread onions over the surface of the dough and sprinkle lightly with the coarse salt. Allow to rise for another 10 minutes. Slide loaf onto the stone and bake for 25 to 30 minutes. Remove from the oven and serve warm, cut into wedges.

## NOTES:

— This recipe is a perfect example of how simple ingredients and methods can combine to make something extraordinary. The dough is absolutely basic, the topping could hardly be easier, but the resulting loaf is far more than the sum of its ingredients. The first time I made this, Fr. Gabriel claimed it was "the best bread I've had in the very long time," and Fr. Ronald asked if I had "done something special with the crust."

— If you don't have a pizza stone, place the loaf on a lightly greased baking sheet (the heavier the better) for the second rising, then continue with the directions.

— You can use other kinds of onions with good results, but I think the red ones look most attractive. If you can't find a small onion, use about half of a medium-size one. You can always use the remainder in a salad. Or better still, double this recipe!

# Sally Lunn

1 pkg. active dry yeast
½ cup lukewarm water
   (100 to 110°F)
1½ cups warm cream
3 eggs, room temperature,
   lightly beaten

¼ cup sugar
1 tsp. salt
⅛ tsp. nutmeg
4 cups all-purpose flour

---

Combine yeast with warm water and stir until dissolved. Add cream, eggs, sugar, salt, and nutmeg. Stir in flour, 1 cup at a time, and beat until well blended—it will form a thick batter. Cover and let rise until doubled, about 1 hour.

Lightly grease two 46-ounce juice cans. Cut a circle of waxed paper or parchment to fit the bottom of each can; place in the cans. Divide dough between the two cans—it should fill them up by about a third. Cover and let rise until doubled, about 45 to 60 minutes.

Place cans on a jellyroll pan or baking sheet and bake in a preheated 375°F oven for 35 to 40 minutes, or until an inserted cake tester comes out clean and the bread is pulling away from the sides of the can. If the tops seem to be browning too quickly, lightly cover them with foil about halfway through the baking process. Place cans on a wire rack to cool for at least 45 minutes before removing the bread from the cans. Then cool completely on a wire rack.

## NOTES:

— There are two possible origins for the name of this light golden tea cake. The one usually given in England is that they are named after a seventeenth-century pastry cook named Sally Lunn, who was, as the story goes, a Huguenot fleeing the persecutions under Louis XIV in France. She settled in Bath, England, and opened a shop that specialized in light tea cakes. She would take to the streets and sell them in a basket. The building that housed her bakery was renovated in the 1930s, and the original ovens were uncovered in the basement. You can visit there today and sample buns made from the original recipe, which supposedly is a closely guarded secret passed on with the deed of the building. The other explanation given for this unusual name is that it is a corruption of the French *soleil et lune* (sun and moon) because the bread is a golden color, but is often served sliced horizontally and the layers spread with butter, clotted cream, or whipped cream. I don't know which explanation is correct, but I know I like the bread served with whipped cream!

— If you don't use juice in large cans, ask them to save a couple of cans for you at a local school cafeteria—soups and stocks come in the same size can for institutional use. Soak off the labels, and remove as much of the glue as possible since it will re-melt in the oven and can make a mess.

— As I was developing this recipe, I once tried pouring all the batter into one can and only letting it rise a little before baking. The batter erupted out of the can like lava from a volcano, spilled all over the oven and fused the can to the oven rack. Learn from my mistake and use two cans, and place them on the baking sheet just in case.

# Swedish Limpa Rye

¼ cup brown sugar
2 pkg. yeast
1 Tbs. gluten powder
   (optional)
3 cups stone-ground rye flour
2 cups lukewarm coffee
¼ cup melted butter

zest of one medium orange, plus
   juice
1 Tbs. anise seed, crushed
2 tsp. salt
2½ to 3 cups unbleached bread
   flour

---

In a large mixing bowl, mix sugar, yeast, gluten powder, and 2 cups of rye flour until thoroughly blended. Pour in coffee and beat for about 200 strokes. Allow to rest for 5 minutes as the yeast develops and the liquid is absorbed. During this time, grate the zest of the orange on top of the mixture and squeeze out the juice into the bowl. Add the melted butter, crushed anise seed, and salt, and stir until blended. Add the remaining cup of rye flour, and stir until incorporated.

At this point abandon the spoon and add 2 cups of the bread flour by hand. Turn the dough out onto a floured board and begin kneading, adding at least ½ cup additional bread flour, more if the dough seems unmanageable. Remember, rye flour dough will be stickier than white flour, so don't add too much at a time or you may end up with a dry, crumbly loaf. Knead for about 5 minutes, until the dough is smooth and only slightly sticky. Rinse out the mixing bowl, lightly oil the surface of the dough, and place it back in the bowl. Cover with a towel and let rise until doubled, about 1½ hours.

Punch down and knead for 2 minutes to work out the larger air pockets and reactivate the yeast. Divide dough in half and form into two oval loaves. Place them side by side on a lightly greased cookie sheet. Cover and allow to rise for 45 minutes to 1 hour. Preheat oven to 375°F. When loaves are nearly doubled, you may use a razor blade or sharp knife to make three parallel slashes in the top of each loaf. Place on a shelf in the middle of the oven and bake for 40 to 45 minutes. Loaves are done when they are crusty and well browned and sound hollow when tapped. They will be heavier and denser than white bread, so don't let that distress you. Cool thoroughly on racks before storage.

NOTES:

— I confess that I don't much care for rye bread, mainly because I don't like the flavor of caraway seeds, which most commercial bakeries seem to insist upon. But the subtle blend of coffee, orange, and anise in this bread is a delightful surprise, like aromatherapy for your whole house!

— There are dozens of variations of limpa rye, so feel free to experiment. Try adding a teaspoon of ground cumin or cardamom, double the amount of anise, or a tablespoon of caraway seeds. Double the amount of orange zest, or try lemon zest instead. For a delicious breakfast bread that makes excellent toast, add a cup of raisins to the dough before the last cup of flour. Consider using a stout ale instead of the coffee. If you use finely ground rye instead of the coarser stone-ground flour, you'll get a lighter loaf with a finer texture, but my monastery brethren seem to prefer the heartier version. You can also use a higher proportion of white flour.

— Limpa makes a great accompaniment to baked ham, or a thick ham and bean soup. Try it as a base for a Reuben sandwich, or just spread it with cream cheese.

— This bread will keep longer than other breads, and it also freezes well.

# American Flavors

# Anadama Bread

¾ cup cornmeal
1 cup boiling water
¼ cup molasses
3 Tbs. shortening or butter

1½ tsp. salt
¼ cup lukewarm water
  (100 to 110°F)
1 pkg. active dry yeast
3½ to 4¼ cups bread flour

---

Combine cornmeal, boiling water, molasses, shortening, and salt in a medium-size mixing bowl and stir until thoroughly blended. Cool to lukewarm. Dissolve yeast in warm water and allow to develop until foamy. Stir yeast into cornmeal mixture. One cup at a time, add 3 cups of flour, each time stirring until thoroughly incorporated.

Add enough of the remaining flour to make a soft dough. Turn out onto a lightly floured board and knead for 8 to 10 minutes, adding small amounts of flour as needed to keep the dough from sticking to the work surface. Rinse and dry the bowl, then oil the surface of the dough and place in the bowl. Cover with a clean, dry dish towel, and let rise in a warm place free from drafts for about 1 hour, or until doubled in volume. Punch dough down. Form into a loaf and place in a lightly greased 9 × 5 × 3 inch loaf pan. Cover and let rise until nearly doubled, about 45 minutes. Bake at 375°F for about 40 to 45 minutes, or until dark brown. Bread is done when it slides easily from the pan and sounds hollow when tapped on the bottom. Cool on a wire rack.

## NOTES:

— I have read several different versions of the story of how this bread got its name, but they all revolve around the idea of a disgruntled husband with a wife named Ana. In some versions he has to make his own bread because she's so inept, in others he's tired of plain white bread and develops his own recipe for the sake of variety. In every story, he mutters, "Ana, damn her! Ana, damn her!" as he kneads the dough. But somewhere I have read another explanation that seems just as plausible: that "anadama" is a variety of corn. Unfortunately, a look in the *Oxford English Dictionary* yielded no results, and Webster's didn't help either, so I'll have to keep looking for a definitive answer. But don't wait for me to complete my research before you make this bread, especially if you like the flavor of molasses.

— Normally I prefer to bake bread in a medium-size loaf pan, that is, one that measures 8½ x 4½ x 2½ inches. But this recipe makes just a little too much dough for that size pan, and the resulting loaf can appear misshapen and is more prone to be a bit doughy in the center. The larger pan is a better fit. But if you don't have that size pan, just divide the dough in half and make two free-form loaves on a single baking sheet.

— This bread doesn't last more than a day in the monastery, with Br. Anthony and other monks coming back to the kitchen for a slice as an afternoon snack. I like to put it out at breakfast as it makes excellent toast.

# Boston Brown Bread

½ cup raisins
½ cup rye flour
½ cup cornmeal
½ cup all-purpose flour
1 tsp. baking soda

½ tsp. salt
2 Tbs. brown sugar
¼ cup molasses
1 cup warm buttermilk

Thoroughly grease two empty 21-ounce cans (the kind that pie filling or fruit comes in—remove labels first). Cut out circles of waxed paper and place them in the bottom of the cans. Plump the raisins in ½ cup hot water; drain and pat dry with paper towel. Combine rye flour, cornmeal, and all-purpose flour with baking soda and salt; stir until well blended. In a separate container, mix molasses and sugar with warm buttermilk and stir to combine. Pour buttermilk mixture into flour mixture and mix well, then fold in the raisins until evenly distributed. Divide batter evenly between the 2 cans. Cover with greased aluminum foil and tie around the top with string (dental floss works, too). Place a wire rack at the bottom of a large kettle with a lid, and place cans on top of the rack. Pour in enough boiling water to come halfway up the sides of the cans. Cover kettle with a lid and steam cans at a slow boil for at least 2 hours, adding more water as needed. Bread is done when a toothpick inserted comes out clean. Remove cans from water and take off the aluminum foil. Allow bread to cool to lukewarm before you remove it from the cans. If it resists coming out, run a thin knife blade around the inside of the can and shake the bread out gently.

**NOTES:**

— Boston Brown Bread is also called "Third Bread" because it uses one part each of three different grains. It is traditional to steam the bread in cans, and you sometimes see old-fashioned recipes that call for a one-pound lard bucket, or a bread pudding mold, both of which would work, if you happen to have them around! Whatever you use, just make sure that your cans are only half filled with batter.

— This is another bread that molasses lovers really enjoy. The small loaves that result from this recipe are dense and quite moist, so much so that you might suspect that they are underdone. But after two or three hours in a boiling water bath, you can rest assured that you've got it right. Slice the bread thin and serve it with cream cheese and baked beans.

# Corn Bread

1 cup yellow cornmeal
1 cup all-purpose flour
⅓ cup granulated sugar
1 Tbs. baking powder
½ tsp. salt

¼ cup butter or shortening,
  melted
1 cup milk
1 large egg

---

Spray an 8 x 8 inch pan on the bottom and sides with cooking spray, and preheat the oven to 400°F. Place cornmeal, flour, sugar, baking powder, and salt in a medium-size bowl and whisk until well blended. In a separate bowl, whisk together shortening, milk, and egg until smooth. Add to dry ingredients and stir until just moistened—the mixture will be slightly lumpy. Pour batter into prepared pan and spread evenly. Bake for 20 to 25 minutes, or until top is golden brown and a toothpick inserted into the center of the bread comes out clean. Best if served warm.

**NOTES:**

— When I was little I used to ask for corn bread for my birthday instead of cake. To this day it's among my favorite breakfast breads, although I'll eat it at any time of day!

— This is one of the few breads that I prefer to make with shortening, which enhances the flavor and texture significantly. However, butter will do just fine, as will ¼ cup of vegetable oil for the more health conscious.

— Our Abbot Philip enjoys his corn bread with whole corn kernels. I'm not a fan, but for his sake I make it that way if there's corn leftover from supper: ½ to ¾ cup of corn kernels is a good proportion.

— This same recipe can be used to make cornmeal muffins, but they need to be baked only 12 to 15 minutes.

# Corn Dog Bites

¾ cup cornmeal
½ cup all-purpose flour
2 Tbs. sugar
1 tsp. baking powder
½ tsp. salt
1 tsp. dry mustard
    (optional)

½ cup milk
1 egg
1 Tbs. oil
12 hot dogs
oil for frying

In a medium-size bowl, mix together cornmeal, flour, sugar, baking powder, salt, and dry mustard (if desired). In a separate container, combine milk, egg, and oil; beat until well blended.

Pour milk mixture into dry ingredients; stir until smooth. Cut hot dogs into small pieces (1 to 1½ inches long) and pat them dry with a paper towel. Heat oil to 375°F. Skewer a section of hot dog and dip it in the batter, swirling it around to coat completely. Drop the piece immediately into the heated oil; use a pair of tongs to pull it off the skewer. Repeat with more pieces. Do not fry more than five or six pieces at a time, and use the tongs to turn them over as needed to fry evenly on all sides. Corn dog bites are done when they are golden brown, about 2 or 3 minutes. Drain on paper towels and serve hot. Makes 12 servings.

## NOTES:

— You might wonder why you have to dry off the hot dog pieces. If they are wet, the batter may not stick to them as well, and the batter doesn't cook as thoroughly. This batter can be refrigerated for a couple of days.

— Corn dog bites are one of the favorite ballpark snacks of my nephew Treygor, who enjoys them at the Dozer Field in Peoria, home of the Peoria Chiefs. I try to catch a Chiefs game a couple times every summer. One year I even scheduled a production meeting for the show to meet in the stands on the third base line!

— This batter will work for regular corn dogs as well. Just pour the batter into a tall glass (makes it easier to get them completely coated), put the skewers through the dogs, and dip them into the batter. You can only fry one or two at a time, and they have to cook a bit longer, but it's worth the wait. These taste like the ones I used to enjoy at the Heart of Illinois Fair as a kid, not the pre-fab ones served in the school lunch room.

# Funnel Cake

3 eggs
1½ cups milk
1 tsp. vanilla extract
½ cup sugar

2¼ cups flour
½ tsp. salt
2 tsp. baking powder

---

In a medium-size mixing bowl, beat eggs, milk, and vanilla together until well blended. Sift in the remaining dry ingredients. You may need to add more flour or more milk—the batter should be about the same as what you use for waffles. Put oil in a 10-inch frying pan over medium heat until the oil reaches 365°F. Pour batter through a large funnel in a swirling or crisscross motion to form the cake. Fry until golden brown and crispy. Drain on paper towels and serve sprinkled with powdered sugar and/or cinnamon sugar. You may also place a dollop of ice cream on top, or use fruit toppings.

**NOTES:**

— Although many cultures have various forms of fried bread doughs and batters, the funnel cake has become a part of American food culture through the food booths at county fairs and local festivals. The Pennsylvania Dutch of German ancestry brought it with them to this country (the earliest published recipe is from Germany in 1879), and it has spread throughout the country.

— Mix your batter in a pitcher so it's easier to pour. Experiment with the size of funnel you use, depending on whether you want a thin, crispy cake, or a thicker, more doughy one. You may have to add more milk if your funnel has a smaller hole.

— You can sometimes find pitchers with a funnel spout, and if you make these often, it's worth it to invest in one.

# Harvest Braid

any dough, enough for one loaf
of bread (see notes)
1½ cups coarsely chopped ham
1½ cups sharp cheddar cheese
½ cup chopped walnuts

1¼ cups peeled, cored, and
chopped apples
1 egg beaten with 1 Tbs.
of water for egg wash
(optional)

---

Prepare dough through the first rising. Punch dough down and knead briefly to expel larger air bubbles. On a lightly floured board, roll out to a rectangle about 18 × 10 inches. Prepare filling by combining ham and cheese in a medium-size bowl and tossing to mix. Spread filling lengthwise in the center third of the dough, pressing it together lightly.

Using a sharp knife or a small pizza cutter, cut each outer third of the dough (the part not covered by the filling) into 5 to 10 diagonal strips, cutting from the edge of the dough to about 1 inch from the edge of the filling. Lightly brush strips with water. Fold strips over filling, alternating left and right, being careful not to stretch the dough. Tuck in the ends of the last strips and pinch to seal. Carefully transfer to a lightly greased 13 × 9 × 2 inch baking pan. Cover and let rise in a warm, draft-free place for 30 minutes or until doubled.

If desired, brush surface of loaf with egg wash. Bake in a preheated 375°F oven for 30 minutes or until golden brown with a temperature of at least 160°F for the filling. Allow to cool on pan for 10 minutes before removing to a wire rack to cool slightly before serving.

## NOTES:

— You really can use pretty much any bread dough for this recipe as long as it's not too sweet. A half batch of Basic White (see page 8) or Basic Wheat (see page 6) will do for starters.

— Try to use baking apples so they don't turn to mush, but they could be sweet or tart. Lura Red, Empire, Golden Delicious, Honeycrisp, and Gold Rush are my favorites for this recipe. When they are in season, you could try this with pears, too.

— No reason to stick with cheddar if you have some other cheese on hand that you like, but sharper flavors contrast well with the apples, as would a mild smoked cheese.

# Hog Bottom Rolls

1 pkg. active dry yeast
¼ cup lukewarm water
    (100 to 110°F)
1 cup sour cream
2 Tbs. shortening

3 Tbs. sugar
⅛ tsp. soda
1 tsp. salt
1 large egg
3 cups flour

In a small bowl, proof yeast in the water. Warm sour cream, shortening, and sugar in a saucepan over medium heat—scald but do not allow to boil. Stir in soda and salt, then cool to lukewarm. Pour into large bowl, and add yeast and egg. Add flour, 1 cup at a time. Turn out onto lightly floured board and knead for about 2 minutes. Cover dough with a towel and allow to rest for about 5 minutes, so the dough will firm up. Divide dough in half. Roll each half into a circle roughly 16 inches in diameter. With a sharp knife, cut 8 wedges. Starting with the wide end of each triangle, roll up and shape into crescents, but the points of the roll should point straight down, like the feet of a pig, rather than curving in. Using the blunt side of a butter knife, make a vertical crease in the thick part of the roll. Twist the last point of the dough to form the curly tail. Place on lightly greased cookie sheets. Allow to rise until nearly doubled in a warm place, free from drafts—about 1 to 1½ hours. You may need to gently re-crease the roll after rising. Bake at 375°F until golden brown, about 12 to 15 minutes. Makes 16 rolls.

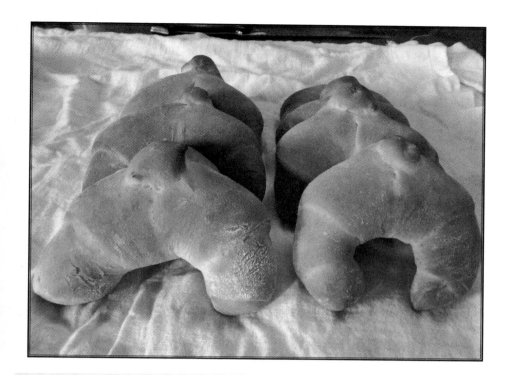

## NOTES:

— I make crescent rolls every year at Thanksgiving. One year Fr. Ronald commented on how one roll quite by accident came out looking like the back end of a pig. With a little experimentation, Hog Bottom Rolls were born! You can, of course, make traditional crescent rolls with this dough.

— My brothers and sisters and I loved crescent rolls when we were growing up, and we still do today. We call them Fred Flintstone Telephone Rolls. They received their name because to us they looked like the telephones on *The Flintstones*. When these rolls were served, it was one of the few times you were allowed to "play with your food"—we would pretend to dial the phone and call each other up using the crescent rolls as receivers. Once when my mom was looking for a recipe for crescent rolls, she searched for an hour in every cookbook without success—because she was looking under "F"! We had become so used to the name we had given them, she had forgotten what everyone else calls them.

# Molasses Corn Bread

1 cup stone-ground whole
    wheat flour
1 cup cornmeal
1 Tbs. baking powder
½ tsp. salt

1½ cups milk
2 eggs
¼ cup (½ stick) butter, melted
¼ cup light unsulfured
    molasses

---

Preheat oven to 400°F. In a medium-size bowl, combine flour, cornmeal, baking powder, and salt; stir to mix. In a separate container, beat milk and eggs together. Add melted butter and molasses and whisk until blended. Add milk mixture to dry ingredients and beat until smooth. Pour batter into a lightly greased 9 × 9 inch baking pan. Bake for 35 minutes or until lightly browned and slightly firm on top.

## NOTES:

— This recipe was never featured on *Breaking Bread with Father Dominic*. I just developed it one weekend with some of my students when we were trying to develop more whole-grain recipes. The result was this earthy quick bread.

— If you like the flavor of molasses, you'll love this corn bread. Eaten by itself, it tastes remarkably like breakfast cereal. Add a touch of butter and a smattering of orange marmalade, and you'll be amazed at its transformation into an elegant breakfast treat.

# Southern Sweet Potato Bread

1½ cups all-purpose flour
1 cup sugar
1 tsp. pumpkin pie spice
1¼ tsp. salt
2¼ tsp. baking powder
2 eggs

½ cup vegetable oil
⅓ cup sour cream
1 tsp. vanilla extract
1 cup cooked mashed
    sweet potatoes
1 cup chopped pecans

Preheat oven to 350°F. Sift flour, sugar, baking powder, spice, and salt into a medium-size mixing bowl. In another bowl, beat eggs, then add oil, sour cream, vanilla, and sweet potato and beat well. Pour liquid mixture onto dry ingredients and stir until just blended—do not overmix. Fold in nuts. Pour batter into a well-greased loaf pan (9 × 5 × 3 inch) and bake for 60 to 70 minutes, or until top is deep brown and a cake tester inserted into the center of the loaf comes out clean. Cool on a wire rack for at least an hour before slicing; it's actually best if sliced the next day.

## NOTES:

— I'm not a big fan of sweet potatoes (I don't like their texture on my tongue) but this traditional quick bread from the American South is a delicious way to use leftovers. Sweet potatoes are used to flavor a variety of southern yeast breads and rolls, too. We sometimes get baked sweet potatoes at supper, so I have the cooks put a few aside after supper for me to peel and mash. One large baked sweet potato will yield around a cup of mashed product. You can use the canned variety, too, I suspect, although I never have.

— If you don't have pumpkin pie spice on hand, you can also substitute 1 teaspoon of ground cinnamon and a generous pinch of nutmeg. If you're a bit more adventuresome, try Chinese five-spice—the star anise in the mixture gives a slight licorice flavor to the bread.

# Texas Moppin' Rolls

2 pkg. active dry yeast
2 cups lukewarm water
   (100 to 110°F)
2 tsp. honey or molasses
1 tsp. salt
1½ tsp. dried crushed
   red pepper

½ cup minced onion
1 cup shredded Monterey
   Jack cheese
½ cup shredded cheddar
   cheese
6½ to 7 cups all-purpose flour

---

In a medium-size bowl, combine yeast with warm water and honey and stir until completely dissolved. Add salt, red pepper, onion, and cheeses; stir until thoroughly blended. Add 6 cups of flour, 2 cups at a time, mixing each time until the flour is completely incorporated. Turn dough out onto a lightly floured board and knead for 6 to 8 minutes, adding small amounts of the remaining flour in order to keep the dough manageable. Rinse and dry the bowl, then oil the surface of the dough and place in the bowl. Cover with a clean, dry dish towel, and let rise in a warm place free from drafts for about 1 hour, or until doubled in volume.

Punch dough down and knead briefly to expel the larger air bubbles. Divide dough into 12 pieces, and roll each piece into a fat oval. Place rolls in a lightly greased 9 × 13 × 2 inch pan (3 rolls across, 4 down). Allow to rise until nearly doubled, about 20 minutes. Bake on the middle rack of a preheated 375°F oven for about 35 to 40 minutes, or until top crust is browned. Remove rolls from pan and cool on racks.

## NOTES:

— With so many different palates to please, our abbey cooks are usually pretty cautious about spicy seasonings. As a result, sometimes monastery food is a bit bland, so I like to create breads with strong flavors. Every time I serve these rolls, one of the brothers is sure to comment on how he expected "just another roll" and got a mouthful of pepper-and-cheese-bread-with-an-attitude. These rolls are actually pretty mild compared to a lot of Tex-Mex food, so feel free to increase the amount of dried pepper.

— Most recipes for rolls use milk to make for a softer, more tender crumb, but I used water in this recipe because I wanted these to be sturdy enough to stand up to a Texas-sized slice of barbecued beef brisket. You can even slice them to make buffet sandwiches, as I have done once or twice for our community night card parties. The spicy taste contrasts nicely with a sweet barbecue sauce, and there's nothing better for moppin' up the last of the baked beans on your plate. If you want daintier rolls, you can divide the dough into 16 or even 20 pieces, but then everyone's going to take two anyway, so you might as well make them larger!

— I used ordinary dried crushed red pepper for this recipe, but if you're the kind of cook who keeps fresh jalapenos or other hot peppers in the fridge, by all means use them. Three 3-inch jalapenos, minced fine, provide moderate heat. You can always experiment with other peppers as well.

# Herbal
# Breads

# Bacon Dill Bread

2 pkg. active dry yeast
½ cup lukewarm water
　　(100 to 110°F)
2 tsp. brown sugar
1 cup milk
1 cup cottage cheese

2 Tbs. fresh chopped dill
　　(1 Tbs. dried)
1½ tsp. salt
5½ to 6 cups all-purpose flour
⅔ cup cooked, crumbled bacon,
　　drained (about 14 to 16
　　strips)

Proof yeast with water and sugar in a small bowl. Blend milk and cottage cheese in a blender until smooth, and warm mixture to 100 to 110°F. Pour milk mixture into a large bowl and add yeast, dill, and salt. Stir in 2 cups of flour until thoroughly incorporated. Add bacon and mix thoroughly. Add 3 more cups of flour, 1 cup at a time, mixing thoroughly each time. Turn dough out onto a lightly floured board and knead for 6 to 8 minutes, adding small amounts of flour as needed to keep dough manageable. At the end of the kneading period, dough should be soft rather than stiff, but only slightly sticky. Oil the surface of the dough and place back in the rinsed bowl. Cover with a towel and allow to rise in a warm place free from drafts for 45 to 60 minutes, or until doubled.

Punch dough down and knead briefly to work out the larger air bubbles. Dough may be formed into one large or two medium free-form loaves and placed on a lightly greased baking sheet, or divided into two and placed in standard loaf pans. (If you make free-form loaves, they may not rise as high as in a pan.) Cover and let rise for 20 to 30 minutes or until nearly doubled. Bake in a preheated 350°F oven for 40 to 45 minutes, until lightly brown and sounding hollow when tapped. The interior temperature should be 190 to 195°F. Remove from pans and cool on wire racks.

## NOTES:

— Dill is not a flavoring I much care for (except in pickles) but our Br. Nathaniel finds it irresistible. Monasteries are like other families—the cook can't always make what he likes best!—so I developed this bread flavored with dill and bacon. You'll often see recipes for "dilly bread" which use sautéed onions and caraway seed for flavor, but I find they overwhelm the dill, so I use bacon instead. You'll notice that there's no oil in this recipe—between the bacon and the cheese, there's plenty of fat to enrich the dough. If you use low-fat or fat-free products, the dough will not be as soft and smooth, but the bread will still be delicious.

— You can fry the bacon, drain, and then crumble it, or you can cut the bacon into small pieces and then fry and drain it. Either way works fine for the recipe, although with the latter technique I find myself more inclined to nibble!

— I often bake this bread in a 2-quart casserole dish, but there's just a little too much dough to fit. So I divide out enough dough to fill a mini-loaf pan. That way I can have a sample loaf for my helpers when the bread comes out of the oven, and the large loaf to serve the community.

# Cheddar Chive Drop Biscuits

2 cups all-purpose flour or
    gluten-free baking mix
½ tsp. salt
1 Tbs. sugar
2 tsp. baking powder

2 Tbs. chopped fresh chives
½ cup vegetable shortening
1 cup milk
¼ cup shredded sharp cheddar

Preheat oven to 425°F. Stir dry ingredients together in a medium-size bowl. Cut in vegetable shortening using a pastry blender or two knives. Add milk and stir until just blended. Drop by tablespoons onto a lightly greased baking sheet. Bake at 425°F for 12 to 15 minutes, or until lightly browned. Cool slightly and serve warm. Makes 12 biscuits.

• • • • • • • • • • • • • • • • • •

## NOTES:

— I've made these plenty of times at home in my familiar oven and at bread demos in a variety of kitchens, and they've always turned out great.

— You can substitute other fresh herbs like basil, rosemary, or thyme. If you're using dried herbs, use only a tablespoon.

— My sister Lisa recommends brushing these with garlic butter just before serving, and I agree!

# Herbal Encouragement Bread

1 pkg. active dry yeast
¼ cup lukewarm water
    (100 to 110°F)
1 cup sour cream
1 egg
1 Tbs. vegetable oil
2 tsp. honey

¼ tsp. baking soda
1 tsp. salt
¼ cup minced onion
½ tsp. dried thyme
4 to 4½ cups all-purpose
    unbleached flour

---

    Dissolve yeast in warm water and allow to develop until foamy. Heat sour cream to 110 to 120°F and pour into a medium-size mixing bowl. Add egg, oil, honey, soda, salt, onion, and thyme, and stir until thoroughly mixed. Add yeast and stir until combined. Add 4 cups flour, 1 cup at a time, mixing thoroughly after each cup. Turn dough out onto a lightly floured surface and knead gently for 1 minute. Allow dough to rest for 10 minutes (this resting period helps the dough to "firm up"). Knead for another 4 minutes, adding small amounts of flour as needed to keep the dough manageable—dough will be elastic but slightly sticky. Lightly oil the surface of the dough and place in the rinsed mixing bowl. Cover with a dish towel and let rise in a warm, draft-free place about 1 hour, or until doubled.

    Punch dough down and knead briefly to expel the larger air bubbles. Divide dough into 3 equal portions. Roll each portion into a rope 18 inches long. Braid ropes to form a loaf, tucking the ends underneath. Place on a lightly greased baking sheet. Cover and let rise until doubled, about 30 minutes. Bake in a preheated 350°F oven for 25 to 30 minutes, or until it's golden brown and sounds hollow when tapped. The interior temperature should be 190 to 195°F. Remove from pan and cool on a wire rack for 15 minutes, then brush the top and sides of the loaf with butter if desired.

## NOTES:

— I developed this recipe as a bread to share with a friend who is going through a difficult time, as several of the ingredients have a symbolic meaning. The sour cream symbolizes making the best of something that has gone bad. The onions of course represent tears, and the thyme is the herb of perseverance and courage, as this hardy plant thrives in the rockiest and harshest of environments. The loaf is braided to suggest that although things in the person's life may look tangled and confused, stepping back and reflecting may reveal both a pattern and a purpose. A fresh loaf of bread with a handwritten note explaining its message would mean far more than any store-bought card.

— You should feel free to substitute sugar or molasses for the honey in this recipe, according to personal taste. The chopped onion could be red, yellow, white, or green, depending upon what's in the fridge. I usually sauté onions before adding them to the dough, but in this case I added them directly and the result was just fine.

— The first time I baked this bread, it was one of those cool evenings in mid-spring when you leave the windows of the kitchen open. You could actually smell the aroma of this bread all the way out in the parking lot by the school gym!

# Housewarming Rolls

½ batch of Basic Roll Dough
    (see page 4)
¼ cup (½ stick) butter, melted
1 Tbs. dried parsley
    (for merriment and
    hospitality)

1 tsp. dried marjoram
    (for joy)
½ tsp. dried rubbed sage
    (for health and long life)
½ tsp. dried powdered rosemary
    (for good memories)

Prepare batch of Basic Roll Dough through first rise. Punch down and knead briefly to work out the larger air bubbles. Combine melted butter and herbs in a small bowl. Divide dough in half (use half for this recipe and half for dinner rolls for your own family!). Divide 1 portion of dough into 16 pieces and roll into balls. Dip each ball of dough into butter mixture and arrange in a single layer in an ungreased 2-quart round casserole dish. Pour remaining butter mixture over rolls. Cover with plastic wrap and allow to rise for 30 minutes or until doubled. Remove plastic and place in a preheated 350°F oven. If desired, just before placing the pan in the oven, you may brush the top with milk and sprinkle with sesame seeds. Bake for 20 to 25 minutes or until browned on top and rolls begin to pull slightly away from the sides of the dish. Allow to sit for 10 minutes before removing from dish, then place on wire rack to cool.

## NOTES:

— Nothing says "Welcome to the neighborhood" like a loaf of freshly baked bread or a pan of homemade rolls. These rolls are flavored with herbs that symbolize some of the qualities of a happy home, so bake them for a new neighbor or for an old friend settling into a new house.

— I'm not sure how the other herbs obtained their meanings, but parsley was served between courses at Roman feasts—chewing the leaves helped "cleanse the palate" for the next dish, and helped to sweeten the breath. So it came to be associated with hospitality and partying.

— For the sake of convenience, I have used dried herbs for this recipe. If you use fresh herbs, use double the amount of parsley and marjoram, but only ¾ of a teaspoon each of fresh minced sage and rosemary. These stronger herbs can be overwhelming when fresh.

—If you think the rolls are browning too quickly, loosely cover the top with aluminum foil, but remove it for the last 5 or 10 minutes of baking. The sesame seeds really do add to the appearance, so if you have them on hand, by all means use them.

# Inside Out Nacho Bread

¼ cup (half a stick) butter + 1
    Tbs., chilled
1 cup chopped onion
1¼ cups yellow cornmeal
1 cup all-purpose flour
¼ cup sugar
1 Tbs. baking powder
1½ tsp. salt

½ tsp. baking soda
3 eggs, well beaten
1½ cups sour cream
1½ cups shredded cheddar
    cheese
⅓ cup chopped black olives
¼ cup minced jalapeno
    peppers

Over medium heat, sauté the onion in 1 tablespoon of butter until tender, about 10 minutes. Set aside to cool. Sift cornmeal, flour, sugar, baking powder, salt, and baking soda into a medium-size bowl and stir to blend. Cut the butter into the dry ingredients using a pastry cutter or two knives until the mixture resembles coarse crumbs. Add eggs and sour cream and stir until blended. Mix in the cheese, olives, and peppers. Pour the batter into a greased 11-inch stoneware deep-dish pizza pan, or a 9 × 9 × 2 inch cake pan. Bake in a preheated 400°F oven for 35 to 40 minutes, or until it's golden brown and a cake tester inserted into the center comes out clean. Cool for 15 to 20 minutes in the pan before cutting into wedges or squares. Serve warm, topped with salsa, sour cream, and/or guacamole.

## NOTES:

— Nachos have become standard fare at baseball stadiums across the country. Usually there's one food stand at the ballpark that serves the best ones, and if you arrive early, finding that stand is a worthwhile activity. This sour cream—based corn bread uses all the toppings that make nachos such a popular snack, but mixed on the inside rather than on top. Normally the monks of Saint Bede are not big fans of Tex-Mex cooking, but this corn bread disappeared rapidly when I served it for the first time at a Lenten lunch, topped with sour cream and homemade salsa.

— This bread is not that spicy, but you can substitute roasted bell peppers if you think the jalapenos are too much. Try to find a good sharp cheddar cheese at the deli and grate it yourself rather than using that bland pre-grated stuff in the dairy case.

# Italian Onion Herb Bread

⅓ cup finely chopped onion
2 Tbs. vegetable oil (divided)
1 or 2 Tbs. Italian herb mix
1 cup milk
2 pkg. active dry yeast

1 cup lukewarm water
 (100 to 110°F)
1 Tbs. brown sugar
2 tsp. salt
5½ to 6 cups of all-purpose
 flour

Sauté onions in 1 tablespoon of the oil until translucent but not browned. Remove pan from heat and add remaining oil, herbs, and milk—set aside to cool to lukewarm. Dissolve yeast in warm water with a pinch of the sugar. Let stand 10 minutes until foamy. In a large mixing bowl, combine oil/herb/milk mixture with yeast, salt, and remainder of mixture. Stir in yeast and remainder of sugar. Add 2 cups of flour and mix thoroughly. Add 3 more cups of flour, 1 cup at a time. About ¼ cup at a time, add enough of the remaining flour to make a moderately stiff dough. Turn out onto a lightly floured board and knead for 6 to 8 minutes, until dough is smooth, shiny, and slightly sticky. Lightly oil the surface of the dough, and place in the rinsed bowl covered with a dish towel, in a warm place free from drafts. Let rise until doubled, about 1 hour.

Punch dough down and knead again for about 1 minute. Divide into 4 to 6 pieces and form into long loaves; place on lightly greased baking sheets. Let rise again, covered, for 30 to 45 minutes, until nearly doubled. Bake at 375°F for 20 to 25 minutes or until loaves are golden brown and sound hollow when tapped. The interior temperature should be between 190 and 195°F. Remove from pans and cool on wire racks.

## notes:

— This bread sells very well at any bake sale, mainly because the aroma of the finished loaves is so irresistible. It's good on the side of any pasta dish, and is delicious sliced into rounds and served with salami and cheese. You can use standard loaf pans if you like (bake for 40 to 45 minutes), but I prefer to make the long Italian style loaves, either on a baking sheet or in the baguette pans designed specifically for long loaves.

— The first time you make this bread, use only 1 tablespoon of herb mix, and see if that's enough for your palate. If not, increase it to 2.

— You can try other herbs in this recipe as well. I made it once with a combination of lovage, savory, and parsley, and the community devoured 6 large loaves at a single meal!

— If you are short on time, omit the onions and just warm the milk to 110°F before adding it to other ingredients along with the oil.

# Pesto Spirals

1 batch of Basic White Bread
    dough, risen once (see page 8)

pesto, either homemade (see
    recipe below) or from a jar

---

Punch dough down, and knead lightly for 1 minute. Lightly oil a 14-inch pizza pan; set it aside. On a lightly floured surface, roll the dough out into a rectangle about 24 × 18 inches. Spread on the pesto, leaving a 1-inch border. Starting from the long side, roll up jellyroll style and pinch the edges to seal them. Brush the edges of the dough with some milk if you have trouble getting the dough to stick. Using a very sharp knife, cut the dough into 24 rolls. Place the rolls cut side down, arranging them in a spiral that starts in the center of the pan and works its way outward, overlapping each roll slightly on top of the one next to it. Cover and let rise until nearly doubled, 30 to 45 minutes. Preheat oven to 350°F. Bake rolls for 30 to 40 minutes or until they are lightly browned and sound hollow when tapped. Allow to cool slightly before serving—just place the pan in the center of the table and let people tear off rolls.

<u>Pesto</u>
2 cups fresh basil
2 cups fresh parsley
4 cloves garlic

2 cups olive oil
4 Tbs. pine nuts or chopped
    almonds
1 tsp. salt
1 Tbs. grated Parmesan cheese

---

Place all ingredients except the cheese in a food processor—coarsely chop the basil by hand first if the leaves are large. Blend on high until you have a smooth pure, long enough for the nuts to be completely ground. Remove mixture from blender and place in a small bowl. Stir in the grated Parmesan. Add more salt to taste.

These rolls have gone through their final rise and are ready for baking.

## nOTES:

— I grow a lot of basil for the brethren, but mostly it goes into pizza sauce rather than pesto. The basil, parsley, and garlic absolutely have to be fresh for pesto to fulfill its culinary destiny—well worth the extra effort. If you can't find (or can't afford) pine nuts, either almonds or walnuts may be substituted, but not peanuts, and in extremis you may omit the nuts completely.

— You may substitute Romano or Asiago cheese for the Parmesan in pesto, but if you do, don't add salt until you've mixed in the cheese and tasted it. Asiago in particular may have enough salt without adding more.

— You can also bake these rolls on two smaller pans if that's necessary because of the size of your oven or your table. I've also arranged them in the shape of a flower, reserving a small ball of plain dough sprinkled with sesame seeds for the center.

# Sage Dumplings

1 cup flour
1 tsp. salt
¼ tsp. dried ground sage (about
    ½ tsp. fresh)

2 tsp. baking soda
1 egg
¼ cup milk

---

Sift together flour, salt, sage, and baking soda. In a separate bowl, combine 1 egg and ¼ cup milk. Blend lightly with a fork. Add liquid to dry ingredients and mix just until moistened. Using 2 soup spoons, scoop about 2 tablespoons of batter and wipe from the bowl of 1 spoon to the next until you have formed a ball; place on parchment or a plate. When they are all formed, drop into simmering chicken stock or soup. They will float on top as they cook. Cover the soup pan with a lid in order to steam the dumplings (a glass lid or inverted glass pie dish is helpful so you can watch them cook). After 5 minutes, check the dumplings every minute until they are done. The dumplings are finished cooking when an inserted toothpick comes out clean.

**NOTES:**

— Sage is the herb which symbolizes health and longevity. I haven't found an official explanation for its traditional meaning, but I do know that you can harvest fresh sage well into the winter—I brush the snow off my sage plants in November and collect leaves for Thanksgiving stuffing. If the plants stay healthy that long, they must have some health-bearing properties! These dumplings are meant to be served with chicken soup, as an herbal get-well offering to a sick friend.

— I was a bit afraid of attempting dumplings for many years, because they are a bread cooked in liquid rather than baked in an oven. But once I discovered how easy they are (and how delicious) I have become a dumpling devotee. The amount of sage in this recipe is quite small, for two reasons: the recipe is meant for someone who is sick and may not be able to tolerate strong flavors, and sage can be overpowering in any recipe, so it's best to go easy. Use no more than ½ teaspoon even for the healthiest diner!

# Spicy Date Nut Bread

1 pkg. active dry yeast
1¼ cups lukewarm water
   (100 to 110°F)
½ cup whole wheat flour
2 Tbs. brown sugar
1 tsp. salt

2 Tbs. vegetable oil
1 Tbs. Chinese five spice
1 egg
3½ to 4 cups bread flour
1 cup chopped dates
½ cup chopped pecans

In a medium-size bowl, combine yeast with warm water and stir until completely dissolved. Add whole wheat flour, brown sugar, salt, oil, spice, and egg; stir until thoroughly blended. Add 3 cups of bread flour, 1 cup at a time, mixing each time until the flour is completely incorporated. Turn dough out onto a lightly floured surface and knead for 5 or 6 minutes, adding small amounts of flour to keep the dough manageable. Rinse and dry the bowl, then oil the surface of the dough and place in the bowl. Cover with a clean, dry dish towel and let rise in a warm place free from drafts for about 1 hour, or until doubled in volume.

Punch dough down and let rest for 5 minutes. Flatten dough into a rough oval about ½ inch thick. Place dates and nuts on the dough and fold the sides over to enclose them. Knead dough to incorporate dates and nuts (at first the dough will be messy and seem to be falling apart, but be patient—it will all come together!). Form into one large free-form loaf or two smaller loaves; if there are dates on the surface of the loaf, push them into the dough so they won't burn. Place loaf on a lightly greased baking sheet. Cover with a clean, dry cloth and let rise until nearly doubled, 30 to 45 minutes. Bake on the middle rack of a preheated 375°F oven for about 40 to 45 minutes, a bit less for the smaller loaves. Bread is done when the crust is browned and the loaf sounds hollow when tapped on the bottom; the interior temperature should be 190 to 195°F. Remove from pans and cool on wire racks.

## NOTES:

— If you like the aroma and flavor of anise, you'll love Chinese five spice. It's a blend of star anise, Sichuan pepper, fennel, cloves, and cinnamon, and it's available on the spice rack of most large supermarkets. In this recipe, Chinese five spice beautifully complements the sweetness of the dates, and the pecans add both flavor and texture to the loaf. If you are a little leery of the scent, use only 2 teaspoons the first time you make the bread, and increase it according to taste. If you can't find the spice, substitute ¼ teaspoon ground cloves, a teaspoon of cinnamon, and a teaspoon of either fennel seed or ground anise.

— As I do with most breads, I tested this one several times, and during one of the trials I was making Kaiser rolls at the same time. Br. Nathaniel came down to the kitchen for a snack and immediately pounced on one of the fresh rolls. But the kitchen was filled with the aroma of anise as well, a seasoning his mother used often in her holiday baking. So before he went to bed, he thanked me, "not only for a delicious roll, but for a wonderful scent from my memories."

— When I make this for my monastic community at Saint Bede, I let the loaf rise the second time in a French *banneton* (also called a *brotform* in German), which is a tightly coiled basket. I generously dust the interior with flour, then place the dough in the basket to rise. When it has doubled, I place a baking sheet on top of the basket and flip it over. The risen dough drops out onto the baking sheet, and the spiral pattern of the basket appears in flour on the top of the loaf. The pattern becomes even more pronounced as the crust browns. I use a round *banneton*, but they make long oval ones as well.

# Tomato Basil Focaccia

## Dough
2 cups tomato juice
¼ cup chopped sun-dried
    tomatoes
1 pkg. active dry yeast
1 cup whole wheat flour
2 Tbs. olive oil
2 tsp. salt
4 to 4½ cups white bread flour
cornmeal
2 Tbs. finely chopped fresh
    basil, OR 1 Tbs. dried whole
    basil leaves, OR 2 tsp.
    ground dried basil

## Topping
olive oil
kosher salt
½ cup coarsely chopped fresh
    herbs (chives, rosemary,
    thyme, etc.)

---

Scald tomato juice in a saucepan over low heat, but do not allow to boil. Add the sun-dried tomatoes and cool to lukewarm. Pour into a mixing bowl. Stir in yeast and 1 cup of whole wheat flour and allow to rest for 10 minutes. Add olive oil, basil, and salt and mix well, about 100 strokes by hand. Add 4 cups of bread flour, 1 cup at a time, until you get a soft dough that is rather sticky. Knead on a lightly floured board for about 5 minutes, adding small amounts of flour to keep the dough manageable. The resulting dough should be smooth and elastic but still a bit sticky. Give the mixing bowl a quick wash, oil the surface of the dough lightly, and place it in the bowl. Let rise, covered with a towel, in a warm place free from drafts, until doubled— about 1 to 1½ hours.

Punch down and divide into two portions. Flatten each portion into a round, flat loaf, about ½ inch thick. Place loaves on a baking sheet that has been sprinkled with cornmeal (you may need 2 sheets). Brush about 1 tablespoon of olive oil on each loaf. Allow to rise, uncovered, for 30 minutes. Dimple dough with your forefinger, each dimple being about ½ inch apart. Mix the herbs with enough olive oil to coat thoroughly, and spread them over the loaves. Sprinkle lightly with kosher salt. Bake at 400°F until lightly browned, about 20 minutes. Remove from oven and cool loaves for 10 minutes before serving.

## NOTES:

— Canned tomato juice will work for this recipe, too, but omit the salt, since commercial tomato juice is pretty salty. Also, the resulting tomato flavor may have a slight metallic tang to it.

— If you have a baking stone, preheat it in the oven, and use a peel to slide the loaves off the baking sheet and onto the stone. The resulting crust will be much better than if you use a pan.

— If you don't have fresh herbs for the topping, use dried and reduce the amount to 2 tablespoons, but brush the loaf with olive oil and sprinkle them on top of the bread as it comes out of the oven. Dried herbs will burn under the intense heat of baking.

— This recipe may be halved, but it's so good, I doubt you'll have any leftovers. The second loaf will also keep well in the freezer for about a month.

# Whole Wheat Stuffing Bread

2 pkg. active dry yeast
1 cup lukewarm water
　　(100 to 115°F)
1 Tbs. brown sugar
2 cups whole wheat flour
3 to 3½ cups bread flour,
　　divided

½ cup chopped onion
3 Tbs. vegetable oil
1 cup milk
1 Tbs. dried sage
2 tsp. dried thyme
2 tsp. salt
2 cups whole wheat flour

---

Dissolve yeast in warm water with the brown sugar and 2 cups of bread flour. Let stand 10 minutes until foamy. Sauté onions in oil until translucent but not browned. Remove pan from heat and add milk and herbs; set aside to cool to lukewarm (100 to 110°F). In a large mixing bowl, combine salt and milk mixture. Stir in yeast. Add 2 cups of whole wheat flour and mix thoroughly. Let this batter rest for 5 minutes. Add 1 more cup of bread flour and mix thoroughly. About ¼ cup at a time, add enough of the remaining bread flour to make a fairly stiff dough. Turn out onto a lightly floured board and knead for 6 to 8 minutes, until the dough is smooth, shiny, and slightly sticky. Lightly oil the surface of the dough, and place in a large bowl covered with a dish towel, in a warm place free from drafts. Let rise until doubled, about 1 hour.

Punch down the dough and knead briefly to expel the larger air bubbles. Form into loaves and place in lightly oiled loaf pans. Let rise again, covered with a towel, for 30 to 45 minutes, until nearly doubled. Bake at 375°F for 45 minutes or until golden brown; the interior temperature should be 195 to 200°F. Remove from pans and cool on wire racks.

**NOTES:**

— My love affair with herbs began when I read Phyllis Shaudys's *The Pleasure of Herbs*, in which she describes bundling up in late November to brush aside the snow on the sage and thyme plants, which may still be harvested for fresh herbs for stuffing. It sounded so charming I resolved to grow herbs on the spot! Two years later I wrote to her to tell her how I had done just as she advised for Thanksgiving that year, and mentioned this recipe. She wrote back asking for an article on bread baking for her newsletter, and the result was a series of articles and a continued friendship until her death.

— This is the ideal bread for cold turkey sandwiches for the days after Thanksgiving—turkey and stuffing in one bite! But don't wait until Thanksgiving—make it for deli turkey sandwiches to take to school or work.

# Index of Recipes